D1471927

Trampships, Tankers and Polite Conversation

Experiences of the Merchant Navy during the 1950's and 1960's.

John Lee

authorHOUSE®

AuthorHouse™ UK Ltd.
500 Avebury Boulevard
Central Milton Keynes, MK9 2BE
www.authorhouse.co.uk
Phone: 08001974150

This book is a work of non-fiction. Unless otherwise noted, the author and the publisher make no explicit guarantees as to the accuracy of the information contained in this book and in some cases, names of people and places have been altered to protect their privacy.

First published by AuthorHouse 9/17/2007

ISBN: 978-1-4343-0526-8 (e)
ISBN: 978-1-4343-0524-4 (sc)
ISBN: 978-1-4343-0525-1 (hc)

Printed in the United States of America
Bloomington, Indiana

This book is printed on acid-free paper.

Dedication

This book is dedicated to the memory of my brother Captain Edward Lee- 1943 to 1996.

I am grateful to my wife Sue, my children James, Jonathan and Katie, my relatives and friends who have had to suffer my stories over the years. And in answer to their often asked question, 'Yes, all my stories are true!' Thanks are also due to Daphne Roberts for her illustrations and helpful comments. Lastly, I am deeply indebted to my good friend John Hughes for his valuable suggestions when proof reading the text of my book.

Table of Contents

CHAPTER 1

Trampships and Hard tack

On the 17th April 1954, a date etched indelibly in my memory, I joined the Merchant Navy as an apprentice deck officer. Up until then I had been a pupil at Boulevard Nautical College in Hull which I subsequently found had prepared me well for life at sea. I was undersized but possessed great energy, with a paper round to help make ends meet and, like many other youngsters at the time, attended Sunday School regularly. Apart from a brief period when I dreamed of being a doctor I had always wanted to be a sailor. Whence this notion came I have no idea but it seemed instinctive and utterly undeniable.

One day I was sitting in the classroom when the Principal, Captain Alison walked in, 'Right, who's ready to go to sea?' I got my hand up first. The very same day I was interviewed by a very kindly Captain. His wife, a gentle, well dressed and quietly spoken lady was also present. I found the interview a little disconcerting because the Captain frequently consulted his wife. My answers to his questions were always followed with, 'What do think dear?' Luckily she murmured the right noises and seemed to approve of me. The following day I signed a four-year indenture as an apprentice deck officer. Among other things I had to promise to be sober and upright. My first wage was to be seven pounds eighteen and fourpence a month. The total for four years was fixed at £500. Strangely, I was also entitled to twelve shillings yearly in lieu of washing soap, which I never managed to get.

Unbeknown to me at the time, I was joining an extremely tough London Greek trampship company. Some people mistakenly called the company

'Lord Line' because all the ships were named after titled politicians who had enjoyed good relations with the Greek nation.

Seeing my first ship was quite a shock. Armed only with its grand sounding name I had walked round King George Dock, Hull passing huge, smart, impressive vessels excitedly reading their names and thinking, 'Is this is it?' After several disappointments I eventually I came across a dirty, rusty ship, which wasn't even floating in water but in a dry dock being repaired. My heart sank as I read its name. This was it; this was the *Lord Sinclair*; my new home. I was very disappointed and in all my years at sea I never saw a scruffier looking boat than the one I was about to board. I was often ashamed that it was flying the British flag.

The *Lord Sinclair* was a trampship - a gigantic seagoing shopping trolley capable of carrying anything, anywhere for anybody. The owner of a trampship is always looking for cargo to carry. On one trip, for example, we carried ten thousand tons of coal dust loaded in America; the next trip we carried hardwood logs from West Africa to the UK. No two cargoes were ever the same and we often set sail empty, in ballast[1], without a known destination. Then, after several days at sea, we would receive orders by wireless telegraphy and set our course accordingly. Consequently, in terms of earning capacity, trampships were at the bottom of the league, poorly maintained, short of paint, providing poor quality food and little overtime for the crew. However, I was able to boast that before I had completed my apprenticeship I had been all over the world.

The ship I had joined, the *Lord Sinclair,* had been hurriedly built in West Hartlepool during the Second World War. Originally a coal fired steamship, she had been converted to an oil burner and was so slow that, on a good day with a favourable current, could only manage ten knots[2]. I cannot ever remember us overtaking another vessel. She was steered by magnetic compass and navigation was by sextant[3] and azimuth mirror[4]. This, of course, was the norm although we had heard of radar, gyrocompass[5] and automatic steering. Satellite navigation had not been invented then.

The ship had five cargo hatches and fully loaded carried about ten thousand tons. She was about as long as a football pitch, which is tiny, compared to the modern gigantic bulk carriers. The metal of which she was constructed must have been of poor quality as nothing would stop it rusting. We used to joke that it was made of garden railings, which was probably the truth. As a young boy, during the War, I clearly remember men and lorries visiting our avenue, cutting off our iron railings and taking them away.

We had a multi-national crew comprising Greek engineers, Arab firemen, British sailors and deck officers. However we also took on Dutch and German crews with a sprinkling of other nationalities as the need arose.

My immediate superior was the Chief Officer also known as the First Mate but for most of the time he placed me in the charge of the Bosun[6]. Another new apprentice called Brian had joined the company at the same time as me and we spent most of our time working together.

We had to work extremely hard and were always given the filthiest jobs. The First Mate put us under considerable pressure and we were constantly urged to work faster and made to run from one job to the next. His proud boast was 'I'll make good seamen of you', and, in retrospect, he did. According to his decree we were either day workers or put on watches[7]. On watches we worked seven days a week and quickly learnt to steer and keep a lookout. On day work we worked on deck five and a half days a week, having Saturday afternoon and Sunday free.

Our very first job was particularly obnoxious. During bunkering[8] in Hull, several hundred gallons of fuel oil had accidentally overflowed onto the deck, spraying onto the gloss white accommodation and about eight feet up the buff coloured funnel. The oil was black, had the consistency of tar and gave off pungent, toxic fumes. Brian and I were given cotton waste, buckets, and gallons of paraffin and told to clean it up. It took us three days to mop up this vast, sticky mess. On the last day the ship was rolling about in the Bay of Biscay. At that point we did not have our sea legs and were unaware of the many dangers of shipboard life. I was working on a grating, reaching up the smooth sides of the funnel. The bucket near my feet was filled with more fuel oil than paraffin mixed with clumps of sodden cotton waste. Without realising it I had worked myself progressively into a dangerous position. Standing on a narrow strip of deck the ship rolled to starboard[9] and with no handrail to hold onto I realised I was going to fall about eight feet. I clawed wildly at the oily sides of the funnel but to no avail; down I went. I was just congratulating myself on landing on my feet when the bucket followed me. The galvanised metal bucket did a somersault in the air and neatly landed upside down on my head emptying its foul contents over me as it did so. The shock was quite considerable and I was immediately drenched and dripping with oil. I had no option but to take off my clothes where I stood. Now it was my turn to be swabbed down with paraffin, starting with my hair. By the time I was cleaned off most of the ship's company had gathered, helpless with laughter.

We spent a great deal of time chipping off rust and painting. Even though the appearance of the ship was awful the Mate and Bosun had very high standards and it was many months before I was deemed competent enough to dip my brush in a pot of gloss paint. We swept out the empty hatches[10] and cleaned revolting fluids out of the bilges[11]. But by the end of the year I could splice a wire, sew canvas, lift a derrick[12], and drop the anchor, in fact anything that an Able Seaman could do. When I became a qualified deck officer I never had to ask a man to do something that I couldn't do myself. I had been well trained.

Mr. Costa, the Greek Second Engineer, bullied me remorselessly. He also bullied the junior engineers and the Arab firemen. One of his more unpleasant tricks, which seemed to give him great pleasure, was to creep up behind a fireman in the early hours of the morning and hurl a wrench onto the metal deck with a great clang. This had the desired effect of nearly giving the poor wretch a heart attack. Sometimes we would hear a great commotion in the engine room and engineers could be seen scurrying in all directions in a state of agitation.

Now I knew Mr. Costa was not someone one would seek to upset. Although not a tall man he was very powerful and thickset. His arms were as muscular as the thighs of lesser mortals and he was clearly endowed with unusual strength, graphically illustrated by an incident which took place whilst we were docked in Middlesborough.

One afternoon he had gone ashore to phone his wife. Waiting for the phone box to become free he strolled about and became aware that a very large coloured man appeared to be stalking him. To be certain he went into a public toilet and as he suspected, was followed by the man who asked him for a light. Without any pleasantries Mr. Costa hit him and knocked him out cold. He then effortlessly picked him up in a fireman's lift, carried him back to the ship and laid him on the saloon table. The police were called and it was discovered that the coloured man was responsible for a spate of muggings. He must have been aware that seamen signing off ships are always carrying large sums of money. However, his encounter with Mr Costa, at least for the time being, brought his criminal career to a spectacular halt.

For some unknown reason Mr. Costa did not like me. One of my duties every morning was to fill the fresh water and sanitary tanks. To do this I had to operate a number of valves and ask Mr. Costa, who was on watch down the engine room, to start pumps and later stop them. He had no authority over me and perhaps having to operate pumps for me irked him. Usually he was the one issuing orders to other people. Every morning when I went down the engine room his abuse became more and more overbearing. I hid my fear of him and remained outwardly unperturbed. I think this annoyed him even more and he began threatening me with a very large spanner close to my face. This was very frightening but once again I did not show how scared I was. His next tactic, along with the spanner, was to order me to leave the engine room, giving me five seconds to do so. For the life of me I could not bring myself to run away from him and I climbed even more slowly than usual. His failure to make me run infuriated him and I seriously thought he was going to lose control and hit me.

At this point I thought I needed help and went to see the Chief Officer. There was no love lost between the Chief and the Second Engineer verifying the notion that oil and water don't mix. He listened at length to what I had to say and, without hesitation, gave me his considered opinion, 'Kick him in the balls!' My God, I thought, that would be tantamount to suicide, and for days following I was filled with the imagined terrors of ending my life in this way. However, something must have been said, perhaps by the Captain or Chief Engineer, because the situation calmed down and he soon he began to ignore my very existence.

Brian and I had a comfortable cabin situated amidships on the main deck. We had a wardrobe each, large drawers under our bunks and a desk with more drawers. The furniture was made of cheap wood but all in all a pleasant room. A very unusual but welcome feature was that we had our own separate bathroom and toilet.

However, like the rest of the accommodation it was infested with cockroaches. They came out mainly at night when it was dark; switching on a light in the night revealed dozens of the repulsive insects and that really gave me the creeps. We invented ingenious methods of catching and killing them but we never managed to wipe them out.

Unfortunately, just outside our cabin bulkhead[13], there was a steam winch[14]. Now steam winches, when in use, make the most dreadful clattering noise. Sometimes in port we loaded or discharged cargo twenty four hours a day. When you were trying to sleep the noise was unbearable. It could be likened to a woodpecker with a steel beak hammering at your iron skull. We had many sleepless, agonising nights.

Metal woodpeckers were not the only obstacles to sleep. Along with other boys on the ship, Brian and I were also the occasional targets of sexual perverts. These pests were not merchant seamen but people we encountered in port areas. Two incidents happened to me in the Port of London. The first incident occurred whilst Brian and I were asleep in our bunks. We did not usually lock our cabin door except when we were working or eating our meals. One night I woke to find a large hand exploring the lower part of my body. Having established I was not dreaming and that I was not the owner of the hand I quickly fumbled for the bunk light. A huge man was looming over me and I recognised him as the night watchman who, judging by the smell of his breath, was much the worse for drink. Now I felt extremely vulnerable lying on my back and I realised that the only course of action was to reason with him. Strangely, he accepted that I didn't want anything to do with him or what he was trying to do and promptly turned his attentions to Brian who, at this point, was still asleep. Brian rapidly woke up and started swearing at the man, casting doubts on his parentage amongst other things. This of course made the man very angry, and he promptly produced a wicked looking knife and proceeded to threaten Brian with it. Realising we needed help, I rapidly fled the cabin and roused two of the biggest men on the ship who happened to be the Bosun and Cook. When we got back to the cabin Brian told us that the night watchman had gone and was probably in our bathroom. He had in fact locked himself in our toilet. The Bosun and the Cook hammered on the door telling him to come out. There was not a sound from inside *and the Bosun, a graduate of the Merchant Navy school of diplomacy, simply roared 'Right, you bastard, we're coming in.'* Almost immediately we heard the bolt slide slowly back and the door inched open. I watched in awe, waiting for all hell to break loose, as three huge six footers glowered at each other. The night watchman weighed up the situation quickly and must have decided that the odds were stacked against him meekly allowing himself to be seized and bundled away. That was the last we saw of him. Having reported the incident to the Captain the next day, steps were taken to ensure he never got a job on the docks again.

About a year later I was involved in another memorable, but unpleasant incident, once again in London. As was often the case, if I was off duty Brian would be working. This usually meant that I would have to go ashore by myself and on this particular afternoon I had gone to a cinema in a rather seedy area not far from the docks.

The cinema was almost completely empty and alarm bells started ringing in my head when a man entered, and after looking around, chose to sit next to me. Sure enough, after a while, his knees began to nudge into mine. I was older now, much more confident and physically stronger, battle hardened you might say. I decided to visit the gents in order to return to a different seat. Unfortunately this plan didn't work because the man followed me into the toilet and tried to strike up a conversation. I muttered a few non-committal words to him and found a new seat. Alarmingly, the man came and sat next to me and the knee tapping resumed. Soon I was sitting in a ridiculous position trying to get away from him. Eventually my patience snapped. What I did next still shocks me to this very day. As I was a non-smoker I asked the man for a cigarette and a light. He hurriedly obliged, thinking he had made a hit. I took a few puffs on the cigarette and gently found his hand; this reinforced his belief that

I was becoming friendly. In a flash my gentle grip turned into a vice like hold and I firmly stubbed out the cigarette on the back of his hand. This had the instant effect of making him scream and he shot upwards, high into the air. Whilst he was up there it occurred to me, in a split second, that he might hit me on the way down so I gave him an almighty crack on the jaw. The shock of all this absolutely terrified the man and he ran out of the cinema at high speed.

Moments later the manager arrived, flashing his torch in my face. 'Everything all right sir?'

'Yes, everything's fine thank you.'

I watched the rest of the film in peace.

Now it always seemed farcical to me that on this dirty, rusty trampship the Captain and Chief Officer would carry out a Sunday morning inspection of the decks and accommodation. Brian and I used to view this inspection with some apprehension. If everything in our cabin wasn't spick and span, punishment would quickly ensue. This was usually in the form of scrubbing wooden decks or polishing brass on the bridge very early in the morning or after tea in the evening. Our preparation for these inspections, therefore, was always thorough.

We'd found that the only place we could iron our clothes was on the top of our desk. One day I switched on my rather primitive iron to heat up and was immediately called out on deck. I forgot about the iron. Ships, of course, are always rolling about and I hadn't really got used to the idea of everything being stored in a safe place. When I eventually returned to my cabin there was a strong smell of burning. To my horror I saw that the iron had fallen over and burnt a huge hole in the top of my desk. Panic! Shock! Three days until the next inspection! What could I do to hide the damage? First, I scraped all the charred wood away and tried to keep it a secret by covering the hole with a book. Next I glued a small piece of thin plywood to the underside of the hole. By a remarkable piece of luck I managed to find a tin of plastic wood. I filled the hole and before it was dry gave it a coat of gloss varnish. The colour match was passable but before the Sunday morning inspection the plastic wood began to dry out and shrink. Part of the top of the desk developed a small concave shape but it still looked quite good. The morning of the inspection arrived. The Captain and the Mate had a general look around and then stopped at the desk. They both looked hard at my repair and I'm sure I saw a ghost of a smile cross their faces. Not a word was said and then they were gone. Relief! But I think my well-kept secret had been leaked.

I frequently heard it said that the Captain and Chief Steward were paid a bonus at the end of each trip, the size of which depended on how low they managed to keep the per capita feeding rate. Certainly the food, which was the same for the Captain down to the deckboy, was awful. The menus were quite impressive and the food was plentiful but usually inedible. The meat was tough and rubbery and assaulted the taste buds. The vegetables were of the lowest grade and fit only for animals. We did, on one occasion, see a carcass of meat being taken ashore after the whole lot had been condemned as 'unfit for human consumption'. The bread, though fresh, was speckled with weevils and the odd cockroach. Any complaints about the weevils were greeted with a cheerful 'Be thankful lad, its the only fresh meat you'll get today'. Fruit and cakes were rarely seen.

In order to compensate for this unenviable diet Brian and I began to buy our own 'goodies' before each voyage. One of my favourites was a huge, expensive jar of marmite which I thoroughly enjoyed with toast for supper. Sadly, I once left it in the pantry by mistake and it was never seen again. The following week I complemented the Cook on an unusually tasty soup. 'Well' he said, ' Some daft bugger left a big jar of marmite in the pantry so I've been putting it in the soup'. Whenever we docked in port, at the first opportunity, I would go ashore and enjoy a really good meal. In tropical waters, and when the ship was heavily loaded and low in the water I learned another trick to supplement our meagre diet. Early each morning I would search around the deck and collect all the flying fish that had accidentally flown on board during the night. I had to be early because other crew members had the same idea. The Cook was very willing to fry them providing there were one or two fish for him. I spent many hours watching these fish fleeing from the ship to determine whether they flapped their wings or not. I decided, as everyone told me, that they didn't flap their wings, but only glided when alarmed.

Mealtimes are quite important occasions on a ship when everyone gets together to chat and have a laugh. Meals were served at eight, noon and five p.m. Brian and I were required to eat in the saloon with the officers and be waited upon by an Assistant Steward. The Chief Officer insisted we work until the very last minute. Then we had to get our working clothes off, get washed, and put our uniforms on. This was very tiresome three times a day. We were also expected to be sitting in the saloon exactly at eight, twelve and five, which of course was clearly impossible. We were always in trouble for being late for our meals. In addition, some of the Assistant Stewards resented having to wait on us sixteen year old lads. We thought it was great. On my way into the saloon[15] I was often mystified to see plates of food outside on the hatch near the pantry. Next I began to notice that our food was cold as well as repulsive. Eventually I realised that one particular steward was trying to spoil our food because Brian and I were always late and he hated serving us. He was deliberately cooling our food down and I wasn't going to allow that. I complained to the First Mate and the spiteful practise ceased. He then reverted to snide remarks, slamming food down in front of us when the officers had left.

The food situation on the ship led to a great deal of discussion, some of it good natured and humorous. Curry and rice, which I had never encountered before was known as 'duckshit and hail stones.' Although I disliked it at first I soon realised its potential for disguising and enhancing the 'Irish horse'[16] from which it was made. Cornish pasties became known as 'Cornish bastards' or 'sealed orders' because no-one ever knew what was inside them. New dish names were invented such as 'mosquito shin bone broth' and 'chicken lips soup'. The sailors claimed that they had seen the Cook shaping fishcakes by rolling them under his armpit. Kippers for breakfast, it was joked, amounted to everyone being given a slice of bread and butter to wipe on a single tough kipper nailed to the bulkhead at the entrance to the saloon.

From time to time the Able Seaman asked to see the Captain to complain about the food. On one acrimonious occasion he asked the steward for a plate of food which he then wolfed down in front of them. He pronounced it as perfectly satisfactory and said that he couldn't understand what they were complaining about. That took the 'wind out of their sails'. The Cook, poor chap, had to endure endless caustic comments. He was, however, well able to look after himself and was liable to brandish a cleaver or a carving knife at anyone who particularly gave him a hard time.

The galley[17] stoves were heated with coal and were never allowed to go out. The watch keepers had the task of cleaning ash out of the stoves and keeping them topped up during the night. One warped seaman, aggrieved about the standard of catering, hit upon the disgusting idea of intermittently leaving his calling card on the galley floor. As one might expect this had the desired effect of absolutely infuriating the Cook and Second Cook. The Cook was able to narrow down a list of the probable culprits but never managed to identify the actual Able Seaman. Nevertheless he decided upon an equally repulsive means of retribution. Each day he scooped up the offending pile with a metal shovel, baked it on the stove, crumbled it up and used it as an ingredient. Then came the end of the voyage and the 'signing off day' when everyone receives their wages and goes their separate ways - often a day when, released from the discipline of the ship, old scores are settled. The guilty seaman felt he had to reveal his identity and gloat at the Cook's discomfort. Several people heard him say gleefully to the Cook, 'You never managed to find out who's been shitting in your galley all trip, did you?'

'No,' said the Cook, 'and you never found out what you've been eating in your soup all trip, either.'

Of course it quickly dawned on the other sailors that they'd been eating the spiked soup as well. Both Cook and Able Seaman had to make a swift departure as they realised that they were in great danger of being lynched.

In leaving the *Lord Sinclair* it would be wrong to give the impression that all Merchant Navy food was 'hard tack'[18]. I was simply unlucky with the Company I was indentured to. As I moved from trampships to small cargo passenger ships conditions improved tremendously and I began to enjoy first class food.

CHAPTER 2

Tankeritis and the Suez Canal Crisis

If life on a trampship was physically tough, then life on a tanker was mentally excruciating. For the next two years my sanity was tested to its limits. At least on a cargo trampship I visited numerous fascinating countries and spent long periods in port. The tanker I first served on loaded it's total cargo of crude oil in twelve hours and discharged it in about forty-eight. Almost all of the crude oil was loaded in the Persian Gulf and no-one ever got ashore. The oil was usually pumped ashore at oil refineries sited about thirty miles from the nearest town or city. All the hard work on a tanker occurred in port when I invariably worked six hours on and six hours off. Thus, if I wanted to go ashore I had to go at the end of a shift and then start work again when I returned on board. Not a very practical arrangement. I kept a diary for two years which showed that we averaged twenty-seven days a month at sea and three days in port. On a tanker you cannot choose your friends, go to the theatre, cinema, or call in the pub for a drink and a bar meal. Your social life is almost zero and your existence utterly boring, akin to being in prison, or even worse.

The *Lord Hamilton* was a modern ship capable of carrying twenty six thousand tons of oil, which is very small, compared to today's supertankers. She steamed at fifteen knots and had radar, a gyrocompass and automatic steering. The accommodation was very comfortable and the food good. Harry, the other apprentice, and I shared a cabin under the bridge and we worked very well together. Once again we were either on day work or watches but, on this occasion, the work at sea was not arduous nor did the Mate treat us like slaves.

The Old Man[19] (Captain) was a seventy year old dour Scot. Six foot two inches tall, back as straight as a ramrod, still possessing all his own teeth and a good head of hair, he rarely spoke and I think my only words to him were restricted to 'Good Morning,' and 'Good Night'.

However, this was to change when some mischievous wag told the Captain that I was pretty adept at cutting hair. I was greatly shocked, therefore, when one day I was duly summoned and instructed to give him a trim. I was completely taken aback and immediately told him that I couldn't cut hair; but he wouldn't hear of it and urged me to proceed. The results were disastrous as, armed with only a comb and scissors, I hacked a trail of steps, ragged edges and bald patches. As I tried to correct my mistakes I removed more and more hair until one side of his head was virtually bald. I waited in horror as he called for a mirror and silently inspected my handiwork. To my utter astonishment he seemed satisfied and rewarded me with a tot of rum. I suppose he thought that it would grow again long before we reached port.

My second customer was the Chief Officer who again would not hear of my protestations. Whilst I was cutting his hair the Second Mate quietly crept in. He took the scissors off me and signalled to me to sit down. I sat in front of the Mate and carried on my conversation with him without pausing. After some minutes realisation dawned and, much to the amusement of the Second Mate he suddenly shouted, 'Och who the bloody hell is cutting my hair?' Once order was restored, and I had resumed charge of the scissors, the task was finally, and inexpertly, completed. I was greatly pleased when I was again paid with a tot of rum. From that moment on, in defiance of my brutal and inept efforts, I came to be regarded as the ship's barber.

The Chief Officer was another Scot who had been at sea for about forty years. For many of these he had been a skipper on a Clyde Puffer[20] and he certainly bore a close resemblance to a character from the celebrated 'Tales of Para Handy.' Slightly absent-minded and with a thick Scots accent, what he was doing as First Mate on an ocean-going tanker I could not begin to imagine. One day we were loading crude oil at Mena al Ahmadi in the Persian Gulf and as usual the air was thick with explosive gas. He gave Harry and me strict instructions to be on the lookout for anybody smoking. A few minutes later he came out of his cabin and onto the deck puffing happily away on his pipe. With a feeling of dread and a look of horror on my face I shouted 'Chief!' and frantically pointed at his pipe.

'Och laddie, my God, what am I doing?' he said as he hurriedly disappeared inside again.

He used to get extremely exasperated and tired when we were passing through the Suez Canal. On one occasion when everything was going wrong he shouted at a bunch of hapless Egyptians 'This Canal is the arsehole of the world!' Quick as a flash one of the Egyptians replied 'Ah yes Chief, and you are just passing through!'

I recall on another occasion complaining to the Chief about how fed up I was. With a kind of sad, resigned air he answered, 'Och laddie, I've been fed up for the last forty years - you'll get used to it!' Strange to say, faced with the tedium of subsequent voyages, I found his comment quite consoling.

The Captain and Chief Officer had had a long association with each other going back to the early nineteen hundreds. One night, fuelled by a few drams, the Chief told me a bloodcurdling tale about his venerable shipmate... One wild night, a drunken sailor, who had a grudge against the Captain, attacked him on the bridge. Now the Captain was a very large, powerful man and the seaman took a beating himself and went back to his cabin. Later, fuelled with more drink, he again returned and fought with the Captain. This time, the Chief told me, the Captain hit the sailor so hard with one blow that he knocked an eye clean out of his head. As you know, drink does strange things to people and according to the Chief, the man came back for a third attempt at the Captain. This time, I was told, the Captain threw him over the side of the ship and he was never seen again. Evidently, an entry was made in the Logbook that a man was 'lost overboard in bad weather.'

A few months after I'd joined the *Lord Hamilton* the Captain retired and parted company with the ship in Greenock. He sailed away on the River Clyde at the helm of a twenty-foot cabin cruiser. I could not help reflecting on the fact that having spent fifty-five years at sea he had nevertheless bought a boat to keep himself occupied during retirement.

Meanwhile we were all very conscious of the fact that we were living on a floating bomb. All the deck tools had to be non-ferrous in order not to create sparks; even our shoes and boots had to be free of nails. Only when all the oil tanks were closed did we feel relatively safe. The oil had to be constantly heated to stop it becoming wax-like and solidifying and, during loading, discharging and tank cleaning there was a constant smell of gas. Indeed some people felt that a tanker was more dangerous empty than fully laden; after discharging, and before being cleaned, about twenty-two separate tanks were full of gas. Oil burns fiercely but gas explodes. During the late fifties and early sixties there were some spectacular tanker fires at refineries in the UK. Not surprising then that tanker crews and shore workers were often extremely nervous.

On one memorable occasion we were docking at a refinery near Swansea and I was on the fo'csal head helping with the mooring ropes. We were putting a spring wire ashore when someone noticed that the chain stopper was missing. This was necessary to hold the wire tight whilst it was being transferred from the windlass[21] to the bollards[22]. The Mate shouted to me to go the poop[23] and borrow one from the Second Mate. This meant a long journey of about two hundred yards and the chain stopper was needed urgently. I was in a foul and reckless mood having been told once again that I would not be going home on leave. I ran aft[24] and obtained the chain stopper. The chain had a rope tail attached to it and rather than carry the heavy chain I put the rope over my shoulder and decided to drag it. The tanks were still closed, or so I thought. On the return journey, before we had even finished mooring up, someone had put a gangway aboard and seven or eight refinery workers had opened up the tanks and were taking oil samples. I was now running at full speed, dragging the chain and probably leaving a trail of sparks behind me as I rounded a corner of the accommodation and right through the middle of the startled shore workers. Their reaction was both rapid and spectacular. The whole lot of them vanished back ashore in the twinkling of an eye, colliding with each other as they tried to get down the gangway first. I paused for a moment, chuckled to myself, picked up the chain and continued 'forud'[25]. I found myself in quite a lot of trouble for that incident but was spared the consequences since it was decided that the oil tanks should not have been opened before we were safely moored up.

Forty-eight hours later we were back at sea and on our way to the Persian Gulf for more crude oil. An empty ship is so high out of the water that the propeller and rudder are not fully submerged and the side of the ship can also act like a huge sail making the vessel difficult to control. To overcome this problem, ballast is loaded in the form of seawater by simply flooding some of the oil tanks. However, once safely at sea the unpleasant task of cleaning out the tanks could begin. Now empty, the insides of the tanks remained coated with a thick layer of black oil; to remove it a machine attached to a hose was lowered into the tank and hot water under pressure escaping through spinning nozzles washed down the oily residue. Simultaneously the engineers pumped the water contaminated with oil into the sea. Fifty years ago the world was unaware of the problems of pollution and the sight of a vessel tank cleaning, with its oily wake stretching for miles behind it, was fairly commonplace. Looking back, what we did was unforgivable but it was accepted practise at the time.

As the machine was unable to reach every corner of the tank some unfortunate individual had to enter the compartments with a hand held hose and finish the job. Harry and I were given that job, probably because the sailors refused to do it. Looking back, what we were asked to do was criminally negligent as the heat from the water created a steamy, gassy, dangerous atmosphere. Each tank had an iron ladder going down some forty feet from the tank lid to the bottom and Harry and I, working together, took it in turns to descend about eight feet down the ladder with the huge hose. We were under instructions to come up when we felt dizzy and change places. I cannot, for the life of me, understand why we were not told to wear a safety line in case we fainted and fell to the bottom of the tank. All I can think is all those years ago safety measures were regarded as namby-pamby and 'non-macho'. As time went by I heard stories of people falling down tanks and being killed. In one case a brave Second Mate lost his life trying to save a man who had fallen down a tank, he had gone down with a safety line hoping to rescue the man, but the fumes overcame him too.

After eight hours of tank cleaning and breathing in the fumes it was impossible to get the taste out of your mouth. As some form of compensation it was the pleasant practise on the Lord Hamilton to receive a free tot of rum from the Chief Steward. His office was opposite our cabin and Harry and I noticed that some of the sailors disliked rum, but would claim their free tot anyway. We hit upon the idea of standing there with a tin mug each and a big smile on our faces. The sailors who didn't like rum just tipped it in our mugs as they passed. A very pleasant evening was guaranteed.

In July 1956 General Nasser nationalised the Suez Canal and the Egyptians took control of it. This led to a conflict between Egypt, Britain and France and the canal was closed to shipping. My ship, The Lord Hamilton, was one of the last to get through before the bombing started. My parents, watching a T.V news programme, saw my ship slowly steaming along in a convoy. Had we been a few hours later we might have been one of the forty ships that the Egyptians sank in the Canal in response to being attacked. Some ships, anchored in the Lakes, remained trapped there for many months along with their crews, which must have been an awful ordeal for them. A British ship did not pass through the Canal again until April 1957.

During our journey through the Canal we tied up in a passing bay whilst a northbound convoy passed by. With little else to do, two engineers decided to have a swim in spite of being warned that it might be unwise. Then, they made a second disastrous mistake; wanting a rest they scrambled up onto the bank of the Canal. Immediately two Egyptian soldiers appeared from behind a sand dune and pointed their rifles at them. The two Glaswegian engineers unwisely attempted to argue with the soldiers and received a few blows from the butt of a rifle, which quietened them down. On board ship we saw what was happening and became very concerned for them. Luckily, the French Pilot, with his local knowledge and a smattering of the Egyptian language managed to negotiate their release. After a heated, incomprehensible discussion, the two bruised and battered engineers were traded for four hundred cigarettes. Cigarettes and spirits could always be relied upon to solve problems all over the world.

Although we didn't realise it at the time the closure of the Canal was to have tremendous implications for us. To send ships to Europe via the Cape of Good Hope was extremely expensive and so for the next year we traded between the Persian Gulf and ports in the Southern Hemisphere. When the Canal was finally opened up again we thought our trials and tribulations were over but even then we didn't return to the UK for a few months, which was dreadfully disappointing.

By the time of the Suez Crisis some of us had already been on board for eight months and it was going to be another fifteen months before we would be able to sign off. As my sea going experience increased I began to realise that men begin to get pretty fed up on a trip lasting longer than six months. They have had no leave, want to see their families, and need a break. In the case of tankers, as a result of the relentlessly monotonous lifestyle, they could become eccentric and unpredictable and other Merchant Navy men regarded them as being slightly 'crackers'. This mental condition was nicknamed 'tankeritis'.

Work avoidance could creep in too. As we had radar and automatic steering, the usual three men on watch had been cut down to two, one man on the bridge and one man on call. Most of the sailors were therefore day-workers and their duties were usually confined to tank cleaning, chipping, scraping, and painting. As they became progressively disenchanted with life, they hit upon a novel idea. At the end of each day, instead of returning their tools and paint to the foc'slehead store, they dumped them in the ocean. In this way the sailors hoped they would not be made to do any work. As it was some time before the Bosun realised what was happening, this strategy was quite effective. Eventually the only job they could really do was to wash the decks down, so they dumped the hose too.

One day, the Chief Officer gave Harry and me the job of freeing off and greasing the huge wing nuts that secured down the oil tank lids. The Chief had managed to rescue a few precious tools which he kept locked in his office, and we were given the last remaining hammer and a pot of grease with dire warnings of what would happen to us if we lost them, or allowed the sailors get their hands on them.

We lifted the tank lids to make the job easier and attacked the rust encrusted threads of the wing nuts. The tank we were working on was filled with crystal clear ballast water. At one point during the day I was viciously battering a seized-up wing nut when the hammer shot out of my greasy hand. A feeling of horror came over me as the hammer began its upward journey and I began to pray that it would not join the other tools at the bottom of the ocean. My prayers were answered but I realised that the hammer was rapidly descending on us and we dived for cover. As it was, we were further shocked when the hammer fell with a splash into the tank. Having survived a possible fractured skull Harry and I were left forlornly staring into the tank. When the ripples had cleared, to our astonishment we saw the hammer balanced on the round rung of a steel ladder about six feet down. The wooden shaft was swaying from side to side and, thinking that at any moment the hammer was going to continue its downwards journey, I plunged headfirst into the tank and retrieved it at first grab. The Chief Officer never knew how close he had been to losing his treasured hammer.

The crew's joy at having successfully consigned all available tools to the ocean was to be short-lived. At successive ports all the equipment was replaced, though the Captain thoroughly resented the expense.

Another way to beat the boredom, loneliness, and homesickness, and to create a bit of fun, was to drink. Unfortunately, as we all know, there is a price to pay in the form of tiredness, vicious hangovers and, sometimes, violence. Some ships were 'dry' at sea, but the Lord Hamilton was not. It was a lucrative business for the Captain and Chief Steward as they made money by selling cigarettes, spirits and beer to the crew. A bottle of gin cost seven and sixpence, rum was eight shillings, whiskey ten shillings, finest brandy fifteen shillings and a carton (twenty-four cans) of beer was a pound. Cigarettes were eight to ten shillings, depending on the brand, for a carton of two hundred.

Considering the length of the voyage, there were relatively few unpleasant incidents, though they remain clear in the memory.

The Cook and Second Cook were involved in some heavy drinking that went on until the early hours of the morning and the standby man had to call them at six a.m. to begin preparing food. As you can well imagine on several occasions they could not be roused and breakfast was late. Everyone from the Captain down was pretty disgruntled about this, so Harry and I were given the job of getting them out of their bunks. Fearing the wrath of the Captain and the officers we always managed to do so. Experience taught us that shaking and generally tormenting them brought them to consciousness but they were quite liable to lash out without even opening their eyes. For this reason it had become common practise to wake a seaman by shaking his foot. If he lashed out at you, you were well out of harm's way. Some mornings the Cooks were completely unresponsive but we knew how to wake them; our solution was to carry them, holding their arms and legs, and lay them on the floor of a shower. It was then simply a case of turning on the cold water and leaving rapidly. This method never failed to work. Another method I found by accident was to light a cigarette and put it in the sleeping man's lips. Instinctively he would start drawing on it and this would wake him up. In later years I attempted this on a heavily sleeping Second Mate who was always late relieving me at midnight. It worked well for some time but one night the burning cigarette fell out of his mouth and onto his bare chest. Never had he woken so fast. After that he hid his cigarettes and matches before he went to sleep. I tried to persuade the standby sailor to use the same method but wisely he would not co-operate. Many a watch I was on the Bridge, fuming until well after midnight, waiting for the sleep sodden Second Mate to appear in the chartroom.

Considering the amount of drinking that was going on there was very little violence but I do vividly remember several appalling incidents. One occurred on the morning of New Years Day, 1957. There were a number of Scotsmen amongst the crew so naturally they had been celebrating Hogmanay. The standby Able Seaman had not reported for duty and I was sent to find him.

I walked into the Sailor's Messroom and reeled back in horror. There had obviously been a considerable amount of fighting. A bloody battle you might say. The deck was littered with broken glass bottles and blood was splattered up the bulkheads. All round the room there were smears, hand marks, and splashes of gore. Lying in various positions, some among the broken glass, were a number of sleeping sailors. They were caked in dried blood from a variety of facial injuries – the result of fighting with broken bottles. I anxiously checked all round the sleeping bodies for serious wounds, but to my astonishment there were none. I left hurriedly, realising it was futile to expect the standby man to turn out so I did the job myself. Curiously, no one asked for first aid and the next time I visited their Messroom it was swept and washed clean.

A more serious event occurred on a voyage across the South Atlantic. At about one o' clock in the morning I was lying in my bunk trying to get to sleep. It was a moonlit night and I could clearly see out of my porthole along the main deck aft to the Engineer's accommodation. I knew there was a party going on because I could hear voices and laughter. Someone left the party and I recognised him as an Irish Assistant Steward. I watched him as he staggered along the 'flying bridge'[26] and I saw a light go on in the Engineer's Messroom. 'What', I thought, 'Is he doing in there at this time of night?' Alarm bells started ringing in my head as I saw him reappear with a great variety of knives stuck around his belt. Almost all of the crew were slumbering happily in their bunks and I realised how vunerable they all were. Hurriedly throwing on some shorts and flip-flops I managed to reach him before he entered anyone's cabin. I had become quite adept at dealing with drunken men and chatted to him in a friendly way, eventually persuading him to hand over a number of fairly harmless dinner knives. Unfortunately he would not part with one wicked, razor sharp, pointed carving knife but ambled off with me following at a safe distance. Unknown to me there was some friction between him and the two Cooks. He went to their cabin, switched the light on and started waving the knife about over their sleeping bodies. I shouted a warning to them that woke them up and they fled with great alacrity. That didn't impress me much and I was left facing this dangerous drunken lunatic with a knife. I started my 'friendly chat' tactic again and eventually persuaded him to give me the last remaining knife. For an intoxicated man he next did a very strange thing: He handed me the knife handle first, himself holding the deadly blade. Part way through the transfer he changed his mind. I was firmly holding the handle and he was gripping the blade. He wanted the knife back and there was no way I was going to let go. We stood there staring at each other, face to face, silent. As I would not let go, he pulled hard, losing his grip and falling backwards. I could see that he had inflicted a serious cut on the palm of his hand. I fled now and threw the knife over the side of the ship to the bottom of the Atlantic Ocean where it could never pose a threat again. The Cooks hadn't just fled, but had called the Bosun and all the sailors. They were appalled at the thought of a man roaming about with a knife whilst they all slept and promptly grabbed the bloodied Assistant Steward and took him away. I went back to my cabin, locked the door, and tried to sleep.

I heard the following morning that the sailors had flogged him with a chain stopper and put him to bed. This Irish lad was one tough fellow and the sailors had more trouble with him during the night giving him several more beatings.

For the next nine months I had quite an amicable relationship with the Irishman and he even apologised for the knife incident. I was completely unaware that, deep down, he still harboured a grudge towards me. On another drinking spree he tried to exact a terrible revenge, but more of that later.

The heavy drinking was not just confined to the sailors. A new Chief Officer had joined the ship and he had a drink problem. The 'Old Man' had stopped his bond but he was still managing to get hold of alcohol secretly. Whenever he was on watch the Captain searched his cabin and poured down his sink any drink he could find. The Chief was committing the heinous crime of drinking whilst on watch. He often started drinking at the beginning of the 'first dog watch'[27]; by the beginning of the 'second dog watch'[28] he was half seas over[29]. The standby Sailor confided in me that the Chief was leaving the bridge for short periods of time, which meant that as we used 'auto pilot' there was nobody on the bridge at all. I was absolutely aghast and told the Sailor to call me immediately if the Chief left the bridge as I could always wake up instantly, step into my shorts, and be there within seconds.

On one memorable occasion I ran onto the bridge and was horrified to see a huge vessel, dead ahead, about a mile away. A mile is a very short distance where large ships are concerned and I feared a catastrophic collision. I ran to the autopilot and put the helm[30] hard a starboard[31] and dashed to the wheelhouse window to wait for the ship's head to swing. By this time I was one hundred percent awake and realised that the vessel ahead was in fact going the same way as us. There was no danger of a collision whatsoever, in fact, the ship was going faster than we were anyway. I felt relieved, foolish and amused all at the same time. My usual tactic was to stay on the bridge until the happy, carefree, tipsy Chief returned. If he came back up the port ladder I would disappear down its partner on the starboard side.

Much later in the trip the Captain had to sack him and he was left on the side of the Kiel Canal in Germany. He was a very sad, unhappy man and asked Harry and I to wave to him as we sailed on. Standing there, all alone, surrounded by luggage, he was weeping silently. It tore my heart out to see a man looking so miserable but I knew I had to steel myself. I turned away, looked towards the Baltic Sea and got on with the job.

The Persian Gulf may not be the hottest place on Earth but during the summer months it must approach it. My diary showed that I visited Bahrain fifteen times as well as other well-known oil-loading ports. At that time, ships did not have air conditioning and we suffered from the heat. It must have been unbearable in the Engine Room and I know the Engineers often stood beneath a ventilator for the whole of their watch. The heat they had to withstand was legendary even finding its way into music hall humour: 'A man arrives in Hell and is shown around by the Devil. He is shown a variety of rooms each one hotter than the one before. Eventually they arrive at the deepest, hottest room in Hell. The Devil opens the door and the newcomer looks in. Inside the room is a group of men playing cards. A voice shouts 'Shut that bloody door, there's a draught.' The room was full of Marine Engineers.

On deck we only wore a pair of shorts. No one bothered to wear even a hat. We became extremely brown-skinned but we were careful not to get sunburnt though no one had heard of skin cancer. One day I had been working on the deck for about twelve hours when one eye went completely out of focus. I was quite concerned, but the next morning it was back to normal. Each day we had to take a tablet to replace the salt lost through sweating. I took the tablet with a glass of water but it always made me feel sick.

During July, August, and September the heat was at its worst. Occasionally men were paid off sick suffering from heat exhaustion. I can still clearly hear Big John, an Able Seaman from Truro, saying over and over again 'John, I shall die, I shall just die.' He was hospitalised in Mena'al Ahmadi, Kuwait and repatriated. He never went to sea again and became a bus driver. Indeed, people did die and one August I saw several people being carried ashore covered with white sheets from other tankers. The casualties were usually elderly, overweight and unfit men.

By the time the voyage was well into its second year, morale amongst the crew was plunging to new depths. When the mail arrived there was often despair and anger. Girlfriends wrote 'Dear Johns' and men learnt of marital problems. One man read that his wife was pregnant and by simple arithmetic knew the child could not be his. We continually lost men due to illness and one or two Sailors would desert every time we visited Australia. We noticed that on one occasion the Polish Second Mate was beginning to act strangely. He began to withdraw into himself, wouldn't speak to anyone and would lock his cabin door. He left the ship in Singapore with a Doctor's sick note.

There was almost no social life on the ship apart from drinking and I was always asking myself why no one organised any activities. We had a library of one hundred books and we read them over and over. One day I had a thought which rather hit me like a sledgehammer. 'Why don't I do something?' I approached the Captain and asked for money to buy cards, darts, dominoes, and a variety of other games. Much to my surprise he readily agreed. In the next port I made my purchases. Back on board I drew up teams and instigated tournaments. I was very gratified to see I had created some fun and pleasure on board ship. It was also a valuable lesson for me on the road to maturity; I had realised, for the first time in my life, that I could be a leader rather than a follower.

In search of some fun and laughter one night, a group of us made a simple Ouija board. We wrote out the letters of the alphabet on separate pieces of paper and placed them in a circle on a small table. We then placed a tumbler on the table and turned the main light out. Each of us placed a finger on the tumbler and someone asked a question. I don't think anyone thought the tumbler would move, so we were stunned into a fearful silence when it began to vibrate and scrape around the table. Such was its eerie movement that after it had spelt out one word we lost our nerve and removed our fingers. Then the accusations began: 'You were pushing it!' 'No I wasn't! It was you!" After some argument we abandoned the activity too scared to continue. No one ever admitted to moving the tumbler.

The Second Captain was a trampship cargo man and so he took no interest in the loading or discharging of the ship. Because the other officers kept changing, Harry and I eventually knew more about loading the oil, and later pumping it ashore, than anyone else. We were told what to do and then left to get on with it. When oil is flowing on board at several thousand tons an hour it certainly concentrates the mind. The trick was to shut a tank off when it was full and open an empty one at exactly the same time. The danger was that if a tank was not shut off when full, the oil would shoot high into the air covering the ship and everyone in the vicinity. Less worrying, if an empty tank were opened too early then oil in the full tank would run back by gravity and require topping up again. Also, the tanks had to be filled in such a way as to keep the ship on an even keel and not listing one way or the other.

To discharge the oil we used our own pumps. The oil was pumped ashore at a much more leisurely five hundred tons an hour. The task here was to be aware when a tank was empty, close the valve and open the valve on a full tank. We didn't find loading and discharging too difficult but just when we wanted some shore leave we were at our busiest.

Two days after my nineteenth birthday I was promoted and became an uncertified Third Officer. This is what I went to sea for, to be a Navigating Officer. My new role was to take charge of the ship at sea for eight hours a day on the eight to twelve watches. I had to ensure that we did not run aground or collide with other craft. I was responsible, along with other officers, for finding the position of the ship using solar and terrestrial navigational techniques.

It is impossible to become an instantly experienced officer and 'learning the ropes' took a long time. Initially I had a lot of support from the Captain. His cabin was sited underneath the Bridge where he could keep a lookout. A Third Mate is given the eight to twelve watch because the Captain is always awake during these times. If all is quiet then the Captain will have a cup of tea on the Bridge and an early night. More experienced Officers take the twelve to four, and the four to eight watches. All Officers can ring the Captain and request his presence if there is fog, heavy traffic or navigational problems. I noticed that the Captain often appeared on the bridge when I was getting concerned about some situation and about to telephone him. Keeping a watch could however be very quiet and we could go days, or even weeks, without seeing another vessel whilst crossing oceans.

Now you might think that these new responsibilities weighed heavily on my young shoulders. In fact they didn't, because I was well trained and could call for support if I needed it. I found it very gratifying to be trusted with the lives of forty men and a very valuable tank-ship for eight hours a day. The enemy that tormented me came from elsewhere.

During my short time at sea I had been all over the world and seen serious poverty and starvation. I was particularly upset to see ragged and hungry children deliberately maimed in order for them to become genuine beggars. On board this wretched ship there was a considerable amount of unhappiness amongst what appeared to me to be decent, honest seamen. I don't know whether it was my age or my sympathetic ear but people came along and told me all their problems. When you are a teenager and a man tells you, for instance, that he is contemplating throwing himself overboard, it is very hard to bear. A new and unexpected pressure arose for me too. I was brought up in a large family and always surrounded by people, parents, siblings, friends and shipmates. My new promotion involved being entirely alone on the Bridge with clicking machines for company. For a substantial part of the day I began to suffer from loneliness. A depression settled upon me and my own thoughts began to persecute me.

I was a firm believer in God, and the teachings of the Bible. My experiences of the last two years, however, were beginning to challenge my beliefs. During the long, dark hours on the Bridge I began a debate with myself about the existence of God. I don't think a learned theologian would have been impressed with my reasoning but the pros and cons were real enough to me. At the very heart of my argument were the sufferings of children and what I considered to be ordinary, decent hard-working people just trying to make a living. I could accept that God might want to punish wicked people but if he really existed he should, and would, intervene to prevent the pain and agony of others, particularly if they were innocent children. I cannot remember how many days or weeks the controversy raged in my head but one stormy night in the middle of a deserted ocean I decided that there could not be a God.

That night the Second Mate relieved me at midnight and I left the Bridge shortly afterwards. My mind was almost numb with the enormity of the conclusion I had just reached. Was I wrong? Would God strike me down with a bolt of lightning? Would I join the Marine Engineers in the hottest room in hell? I did not think so, but I was about to get a hair-raising shock. Entering my cabin I was surprised to see what looked like someone sleeping in my bunk. Closer inspection revealed a full sized effigy made out of my uniform. An empty bottle of rum lay on the pillow near the head in a drinking position. Most startling of all was a placard, which proclaimed 'The Wages of Sin is Death'. I recoiled in horror thinking that God hadn't wasted much time in sending me a message! But common sense prevailed and I decided this was just an incredible coincidence. This wasn't the hand of God but the work of some of my warped but well-intentioned shipmates. Looking back, was I of sound mind? I think I must have been. Over the next few days I never wavered or doubted my decision and the issue troubled me no more. No one ever confessed to having manufactured the dummy.

In September 1957, a few months after the Suez Canal re-opened, we finally returned to Falmouth. For Harry and I, what had been a twenty three-month ordeal was over- but not quite. Of the original crew of forty-two, six of us remained. Harry and I had each spent seven months fulfilling the duties of the Third Mate. We had been led to believe that we would be suitable remunerated, but when we received our wage slips we were utterly devastated to see that we had not received one extra penny. We immediately went to see the Captain but he fobbed us off with the excuse that the decision had been taken at Head Office. We were both disappointed and furious. We were members of the 'Merchant Navy and Airline Officers Association' and approached them for help. They exchanged letters with the Company for some six months but to no avail. We were finally told that because we had never signed on the 'Ship's Articles' as 'Uncertified Third Officer' in law we were not entitled to any extra pay. How disgraceful was that?

Most of the crew, Harry and I included, left Falmouth and took a night train to London. Amongst the passengers was the Irishman of the knife incident and his best friend. Unknown to me, he was bent on revenge. They had bought a bottle of whisky and some small tot glasses. At about eleven p.m. they arrived, slightly worse for the drink, in our compartment. Paddy, as we knew him, said he would like to have a drink with us. It was the end of the trip and, not wishing to be unsociable, Harry and I readily agreed.

What happened next was totally unexpected.

Paddy poured me a tot and then, quick as a flash, threw it in my face. I was totally blinded by the neat whisky and whilst I was frantically rubbing my burning eyes Paddy removed a bulb from the carriage light and tried to break the glass. I knew exactly what the 'clink clink' sound was and I also knew that once it was broken it would immediately be rammed into my face. By some miracle, the glass refused to break and I finally managed to see again and a violent argument broke out. I knew that I was going to have to fight this mad Irishman and also that I would not stand a chance in this small railway compartment. I needed space where I could use my speed and agility to keep me out of trouble. Grammar School had provided me with some experience of boxing so I knew that my punches never hurt anyone. I persuaded Paddy to leave the compartment and fight in the space between the two carriages. He set off first, me second, and his best friend behind me. I found out that life is full of surprises. On the short walk his friend tapped me on the shoulder and with some sense of trepidation, I turned my head, half expecting that I was going to get a powerful crack on the jaw. To my astonishment his friend said to me 'John, that was a dirty trick with the whisky and the bulb, get out of the way, I'll deal with him.' There then started an almighty slugging match between Paddy and his best friend. This resulted in some innocent passengers screaming and having hysterics.

At the next station the Police came on board and calmed the situation. I explained to them who was causing all the trouble and asked to have Paddy removed from the train but they refused. For the remainder of the journey the Police boarded the train at every station we stopped at. It was a dreadful, sleepless night. However, Paddy was one tough, determined fellow and he hadn't finished with us yet. In the early hours of the morning a cabin boy arrived with a message telling us that Paddy was going to 'beat us up' on the platform when we arrived in London. Upon arrival Harry and I rapidly put our luggage in a pile on the platform. It was five a.m. and we were cold, tired and miserable. We stood ready as if guarding our luggage and waited...and waited... and waited. To our immense relief no one came to fight and we never saw Paddy or his friend again.

I finally arrived in my home town of Driffield, in East Yorkshire. I had been in semi-tropical and tropical weather for the best part of two years. No matter how I tried I just could not get warm and I was soon struck down with flu. I spent most of my short leave bedridden. When I finally recovered I received a telegram sending me back to sea again. I'd had twenty days leave after a two year trip, most of it ill with flu. I was not given to self-pity or weeping but it was with a heavy heart that I set off to join a ship in Glasgow.

I arrived in Greenock on the Clyde and found at last my luck had changed. My ship was brand new. I was also officially signed on as an Uncertified Third Officer and my written indenture was terminated by mutual agreement as, technically, I was still an indentured apprentice with seven months to complete.

By curious chance, in charge of the ship was the same Captain as on my first voyage. When I reported myself on board, the first thing he said to me was 'When I last signed you off I overpaid you by five shillings and sixpence.' I was flabbergasted by this unexpected greeting but he never attempted to recover the money.

Chapter 3

Watch keeping and Cargo-work

Life at sea sailing between ports could be fascinating and idyllic but also tedious and, sometimes, very uncomfortable. Depending upon one's location the weather could vary between wonderful, sunny, tropical days or the ship rolling violently in a North Atlantic gale.

I never tired of watching huge albatrosses gliding just a few feet above my head when I was on the Bridge. These huge seabirds would accompany the ship for days or sometimes weeks; with a wingspan of ten feet they flew effortlessly and so close that you felt you could reach up and touch them. Apart from the occasional albatross it is unusual to see birds in the middle of oceans. The sight of birds is usually a sign that the ship is nearing land. I well remember watching an exhausted bird down wind trying to reach the ship in a fierce storm. The wind was on the beam[32] and blowing at force eleven or twelve. I realised that the bird was fighting for its life. It was slowly getting closer to the ship, sometimes being blown back but somehow managing to close the gap. It had reached within five or six yards of the foredeck and must have been selecting a landing area. Suddenly, exhausted by the effort, its poor heart gave out and I was shocked to see it plummet like a stone into the ocean. I was saddened that its brave struggle was to no avail.

No one would fail to be impressed by the antics of shoals of porpoises. Spotting a ship they would come charging across the sea and play around the bows. Assuming a ship's speed of fifteen knots the porpoises could easily zigzag across the bows all the while leaping high out of the water. Suddenly, as if tiring of the game, and responding to some unseen signal they would all rush off towards the horizon. I have been told that they can give the same performance around the bow of a warship, doing twenty-five and even thirty knots.

Just as spectacular is sailing close to, or through, a school of whales. Watching their huge tails rear out of the water and crash down with a great splash is an awe-inspiring sight. The words 'There she blows!' spring to mind and it always seemed to me that the whale was blowing water up like a fountain when in reality the great creature was just exhaling air. Being born in Hull, and not all that far from Whitby, I knew something of the whaling industry. How they hunted whales in the Arctic Circle on wooden sailing ships is hard to comprehend, but I can well understand how the phrase 'wooden ships but iron men' came about.

Sometimes ships need to stop at sea to carry out engine repairs. On one memorable occasion we hove to[33] in the Indian Ocean. In a very short space of time great brutes of sharks surrounded the ship. It gave one rather unpleasant thoughts of what would be in store if the ship were to sink. It quickly became apparent that the sharks were waiting for any food that might be thrown overboard. Soon some of the crew had made makeshift fishing lines out of rope and meat hooks. The Cook supplied some tough pieces of meat and the sport began. Strangely enough they were not all that hard to hook but they usually fell off when being hauled on board. An Engineer did manage to land a six footer which seemed to give up without a fight. A couple of hours later he asked someone to take his photograph whilst he was holding its jaws apart. He was smiling proudly when all of a sudden the shark's jaws snapped shut. You have never seen a man move so fast. Later we examined the contents of its stomach and we were surprised to find bits of carrot and cabbage.

On another occasion we were anchored off the West African coast waiting to enter port. We had noticed a number of large venomous sea snakes swimming close by. An Engineer decided he was going to catch one, so whilst on duty he made a simple, but effective, metal trident. To this he tied a long piece of rope and in a short while he had managed to spear a six-foot snake. He hauled it on board only to find out that the snake was furious and far from dead. Once again men moved very quickly when the snake wriggled free of the prongs. Luckily for us the creature knew where safety was and slithered over the side.

My fishing skills were legendary, not because I managed a good catch but because I consistently caught nothing at all. One Saturday afternoon, tied up to a jetty in Mombasa, Kenya, everyone was having great time fishing. One chap landed a deadly stone fish but luckily someone knew exactly what it was and it was carefully returned. Someone else hooked a fish, which was attacked by another fish as it was hauled to surface. When it was pulled out of the water it had some chunks bitten out of it and the bites were so neat and clean it looked as though someone had used a razor sharp knife. As everyone was having such success I was encouraged to have a go. After about half an hour, when fish were being caught all around me, I got a nibble. Everyone stopped to view this momentous occurrence and gave me copious advice and encouragement. When the fish again nibbled at my bait I gave the line a vicious tug, hoping to hook the fish. Success! Something was struggling on the end of my line. Everyone watched to see the first fish I had ever caught. Eagerly I hauled the fish up from the depths but when it was nearing the surface I began to think that it had a strange appearance. As it landed on the deck, howls of laughter went up. The hook was pierced through its tail and I realised I must have impaled it as it was swimming past my bait. Since then I have been on many fishing trips. Men, women and children using identical rods, lines, hooks and bait as mine have caught numerous fish but for some curious reason I cannot catch anything.

One of the most unforgettable experiences of my life was to sail down the Great Barrier Reef. This gigantic physical feature is more than one thousand, two hundred and forty miles in length, and comprises two thousand and nine hundred separate reefs and nine hundred and forty islands. There is a vast number of species of coral, molluscs, turtles, fish, seabirds and mammals within this habitat. To give a better idea of its size, it took our ship seventy-two hours to travel the length of the Reef moving at a speed of seventeen miles an hour. It lies between the latitudes of ten and twenty-five degrees south so the weather is stunning along with the clear blue seawater, azure skies and endless tropical islands. I understand the colour of the vegetation varies with the changing seasons, but I saw it at its best. The verdant trees and shrubs, the clean golden beaches appeared to be a tropical paradise. We passed so close to some of the islands that I thought it would be a great adventure to jump overboard and to swim ashore. But, as always, common sense prevailed. The sea was infested with sharks and salt-water crocodiles and life as a hermit on a deserted island would rapidly lose its appeal after a few months.

Watch keeping by day was more interesting than watch keeping by night. Most of the crew were up and working so there were plenty of people to talk to. If the vessel was coasting I would be kept busy avoiding collisions and continually checking the position of the ship. Some skippers liked to coast ten or twenty miles off the coastline but others could be described as 'rock-dodgers.' Coasting very close to the shoreline really kept you on your toes. Frequently altering course and taking bearings of terrestrial objects certainly heightened one's concentration.

Crossing seas and oceans was more relaxed. Few ships would be seen and the position of the ship would be determined by solar navigation. At noon it was a tense time when the Captain would ask me and the Second Mate to read out what we had calculated as the position of the ship in terms of longitude and latitude. He would then read out his figures. There was no room for much error. A navigating officer would soon lose his credibility if his position were wrong. I am relieved to say that I was never involved in a collision with another vessel, nor was I ever shipwrecked. However, there were some interesting encounters which continue to live in the memory.

One day, in the vicinity of Cape Town, I went up on the Bridge to relieve the Second Mate so that he could go and get his dinner. It was flat calm, sunny and perfectly clear. As I entered the wheelhouse I saw, to my horror, a large trawler very close, disappearing under our bow. I shouted for the Second Mate who was in the Chartroom. I knew that a collision was imminent and my knees began to tremble. I also knew that if we hit the fishing vessel it would simply be rolled over and we would run right over the top of it. The Second Mate, hearing the urgency in my voice rapidly appeared. By the time he reached the Wheelhouse window we could only see the tips of its masts above the fo'csal head[34]. Luckily the collision never occurred. Did we miss the trawler by inches or yards? I don't know but it then passed rapidly down our starboard side. The men on its bridge shouted abuse and obscenities at us. To my astonishment the Second Mate was completely unfazed and gave them a contemptuous two armed 'V' sign and left the Bridge without a word. I was left, still shaking, pondering about the mystery of human nature. To be fair to the Second Mate, because the trawler was crossing our bows from the port side, it was its obligation to keep out of our way. However if it was fishing it was our responsibility to keep out of its way. It did not appear to have any nets or lines out and it was not displaying its fishing signals. Most merchant seamen are of the opinion that fishermen are a law unto themselves. They may hoist flags and signals that stay up permanently, or may not display anything at all, therefore when sighting a fishing fleet the onus is upon those aboard the merchant vessel to decide what they may be up to.

On another occasion I had again taken over from the Second Mate so that he could go for his dinner. We were steaming north east in the Bay of Bengal, heading towards Chittagong in Bangladesh. The Second Mate smiled wryly at me as I walked into the Wheelhouse. I looked around the horizon and soon realised why he was amused. Ahead of us was the biggest fishing fleet I had ever seen. The horizon was just a forest of masts. 'You're going to have fun,' said the Second Mate chuckling as he left the Bridge. In hindsight I should have put a man on the wheel[35] and put the engines on standby. I knew that if I rang the telegraph[36] the Old Man would come running on the Bridge very concerned. I decided I would do the alterations of course myself using the automatic steering machine. The next half-hour was incredibly hectic. The trouble with fishing vessels is that you don't always know what to do for the best. You don't like to cross their bow and you don't like to cross their stern because you might foul, cut their nets or lines. A wide berth[37] is the best policy but on this occasion was not possible. I made numerous alterations of course; some right angle turns, some even greater. I had the vessel weaving all over the sea. The wake[38] of a ship tells the Officer on the Bridge and the Captain an awful lot. Sometimes it can indicate the ability of the man on the wheel. It can bring about caustic comments such as 'Are you trying to sign your name in the wake of the ship?' I was very conscious of the fact that the Captain was also eating his dinner and had a very good view of the ship's wake. Later the Second Mate told me that both the Old Man and the Chief Officer were eyeing up the wake but not a comment was made. I think that the Captain had more faith in me than I had in myself. By the time the Second Mate returned I was a dithering wreck but we were through the fleet all unscathed.

Most seamen are quite fascinated by submarines, probably because of the havoc they wrought during the Second World War. They are small, sinister craft mainly concerned with the destruction of other vessels on the high seas. One morning I arrived on the Bridge at eight a.m; we were heading up the English Channel in good weather and the Officer on the Bridge briefed me about the prevailing situation. The Chief Officer told me that we were very slowly overtaking a submarine which was dead ahead.

Was it Russian, British? It was impossible to tell, as, understandably, they are reluctant to reveal their identity.

Later in the morning I received some requests from below to 'pass it close.' I think that some of the Engineers wanted to try out their new binoculars recently purchased cheaply in Aden. I was watching the submarine very carefully and it was apparent that eyes on the conning tower were watching me too - and they were not happy. I crept up towards its stern and nudged our ship slightly to starboard. An overtaking vessel is obliged to keep out of the way of the vessel being overtaken. I was now passing the submarine as close as I thought that good seamanship would allow. When I had it on the port beam it suddenly made a right angled turn and left us. Looking at the chart, I thought it must be British and had headed off towards Portsmouth. I thought no more about it.

When we reached the Port of London there was a very curt letter waiting for me. The letter from the British Admiralty was addressed to the 'Officer of the Watch.' The gist of the letter was that 'it was very uncomfortable to be in such a small submarine and to be borne down upon by a very large vessel' and that 'in future, I 'should give all warships a wider berth.' The submarine turned out to be the HMS Thermopylae. The Captain had a copy too and I asked him if I should write a reply. Luckily for me, he had watched as I had passed the submarine and he was of the opinion that I had maintained a safe distance. He also pointed out that if the Commander of the submarine had felt I was getting too close for comfort, why had he not decided to take evasive action earlier. More likely, we thought the Royal Navy just did not want merchant ships too close to their vessels for security reasons. The Captain wrote a reply on my behalf and that was the end of the matter.

One of sailors' greatest concerns is the possibility of a fire in the cargo. Dockers all over the world are notorious for smoking whilst working down the hatches. I was once serving on a brand new ship on a voyage from Australia to the U.K. This ship was fitted with a clever smoke-detecting device which worked by taking samples of air being drawn through pipes from compartments all over the ship. The pipes all led to a central console and an alarm would sound if smoke were detected. The Officer on duty would then go to the console and examine labelled pipes to see which one had smoke issuing from it. The dockers would be totally astonished when an Officer would appear and claim that someone was smoking. The previous time-honoured method was simply to go down the hatches and sniff.

We left our new, impressive smoke-detecting machine running even when at sea. A few days after leaving Australia the alarm sounded at two a.m. The Second Mate ran to the console but could not find any smoke issuing from the pipes. He woke up the Captain who roused the rest of us. We all dashed around with keys and torches sniffing frantically in all of the compartments on the ship. About an hour later we all got back to bed exhausted, having found nothing. For the next two weeks the wretched alarm sounded at all hours of the day and night. The Captain was convinced that part of our cargo was smouldering somewhere. We made numerous searches of the whole ship, our nerves were in tatters. When we got back to the U.K. the manufacturers told us that the unit was working perfectly and that specks of dust could set the alarm off. We had no more problems with it - but that might have been due to the fact that we didn't switch it on again.

One normally thinks of the Mediterranean as being warm and tranquil, with visions of glassy calm seas and cloudless blue skies appearing in the mind. On a winter voyage from Baniyas, Syria to Marseille that vision was well and truly shattered. The weather began to deteriorate as soon as we left Syria. The temperature dropped, the wind became stronger and the seas built up. In order to control the empty ship we continually took on more seawater ballast. By the time we were nearing France the tanker was nearly half loaded with seawater. The strength of the wind was unbelievable. I remember I had difficulty in keeping my lips closed around my teeth. Seawater was freezing to the ship's sides and we were becoming encased in ice.

Nearing Marseille we picked up a pilot in appalling conditions. I had been sent down to the main deck to escort him up to the Bridge. After a difficult climb up the pilot ladder he stepped onto the icy deck and executed the most astonishing somersault. His pride rather than his person being hurt, he subjected me to a hysterical tirade of Gallic abuse. Having just witnessed his stunning, unexpected acrobatics I could barely keep a straight face. He was firmly of the opinion that we should have gritted the deck for him.

The French Pilot had considerable difficulty getting us safely into port even with the help of two tugs. He was an excitable little man rushing from one wing of the Bridge to the other, sending frequent signals to the tugs by means of the ship's whistle. Even before the tugs could carry out one manoeuvre he sent them another signal for something else. The Captain was a taciturn man, particularly browned off with our difficult voyage. He was watching the pilot's performance with cold disdain, grimacing every time the pilot blew the ear-shattering whistle. Two levers connected to wires opened the valves, which operated the ship's whistle, which was mounted on the funnel. We had found that the levers were very difficult to operate so we had extended them with metal pipes. Now most people pulled on the pipe with one hand but the pilot, being a small chap, was using both hands and reaching above his head. Unfortunately one of his more energetic pulls on the lever caused the wire to break. The metal pipe, now with no resistance, rapidly descended and hit him very hard on the top of his head. This felled him to the deck just as if he had been coshed. The Captain looked at me and smiled broadly with a look of great satisfaction on his face. I could barely contain myself. The pilot was saved from serious injury by his huge hat, but his mood became more evil than before. We were now both subjected to a stream of incomprehensible abuse, which considerably lifted our spirits. Life was worth living after all.

I used to find watch keeping at night more tedious than by day. I would often spend four hours on the Bridge without speaking to a soul and it took me years to become at peace with my own company. Close to the coastline I would be kept quite busy obtaining the ship's position using the radar or by taking bearings of lighthouses. Crossing oceans, it is possible to ascertain the ship's position using stars and planets. To do this one needs to be able to see the horizon fairly well; the only time that the stars, planets and the horizon are visible is at dawn and dusk. The Chief Officer is on watch at these times. The Pole Star is however useful on all night-time watches to check the accuracy of the compass.

To learn about stars you first need to learn the names of the constellations, invented by poets, farmers, and astronomers over the last six thousand years. A constellation is a pattern of stars forming a picture. Well known examples are the Plough, Orion, the Hunter, and the Southern Cross. Once you can recognise the constellations you can begin to identify the stars that are part of the pattern. To complicate matters you see different constellations depending on the time of night or where on Earth you are viewing the sky. As the Earth is rotating as it orbits the Sun, the view you see above is constantly changing. Star charts help you to make sense of it all. Planets orbit the Sun like the Earth does and only half a dozen are visible to the naked eye. Stars twinkle but planets shine with a steady light. Venus, Mars, Jupiter and Saturn are often conspicuous in the sky but an almanac is often needed to establish the time at which they are visible.

The Bridge of a ship in the middle of the ocean is a good place to familiarise yourself with the night sky because there is no extraneous light and nothing to obstruct your view. Once I was familiar with the constellations and the main stars I was always impressed with the thought that ancient civilisations had stared in awe at the same scene. Eventually

I began to experience the night sky as being friendly and reassuring, a feeling of 'all's right with the world and everything is as it should be.' With the uninterrupted view of the sky, meteors or shooting stars were the spectacular light show of every watch.

One night at about eleven p.m. we were steaming east in the Arafura Sea, north of Australia, when a puzzling thing happened. I was standing on the wing of the Bridge keeping a lookout. There were no ships about and the land was some considerable distance away. I noticed the stars spinning around above me. A year or two previously I might have thought that the man on the wheel had fallen asleep but we had automatic steering. I ran into the wheelhouse and found that the automatic steering machine had put the rudder hard over. The ship was turning in a huge circle. I blew the whistle for the standby man to report to the Bridge and changed from automatic steering to manual, attempting to get the ship back on an easterly course. The sailor took over the wheel, which gave me time to think. I could see the Southern Cross and so I knew we were still turning in a circle and that we were not on the correct course. Suddenly the penny dropped; it was not the automatic steering that was faulty, it was the gyrocompass that had failed. Originally the automatic steering had tried to follow the gyrocompass as it swung around; now the man on the wheel was trying to do the same thing. I quickly instructed him to steer by magnetic compass and we were soon back on course. Had we been 'rock-dodging' on the Australian coast I might have been relating a very different story. I informed the Captain, who came on the Bridge to check things over. During the night the Second Mate, who was responsible for the gyrocompass, carried out repairs and the situation returned to normal.

As a way of relieving boredom on the eight to midnight watch, I used to communicate with other ships using Morse Code on an Aldis Lamp. It also proved to be a useful way of honing up my expertise in using visual Morse Code - a vital skill at sea since ships were not equipped with VHF radio at that time. The Aldis Lamp was very powerful and I was easily able to establish contact with other ships more than fifteen miles away. I experimented with other lights and found that I could communicate with other craft up to five miles away using an average sized hand-held torch with a press button. There was a standard way of communicating, which usually began 'What ship?' 'Where bound?' It was always exciting when I sighted a huge passenger liner.

One night, crossing the North Atlantic, I saw some very bright lights on the horizon on the port bow. Bright lights, as well as the usual navigation lights, nearly always meant that it was a passenger liner. When the ship was closer I called them up and received a prompt and thrilling response. 'Queen Elizabeth, New York to Southampton.' At that time she was the largest passenger ship in the world, at one thousand and thirty-one feet in length, capable of twenty-eight and a half knots. I was serving on a cargo ship called the *King William*. I proudly signalled to her 'King William, Fowey to Portland Maine.' The *Queen Elizabeth* wished me 'Bon Voyage' and 'Good night' and I replied in a similar fashion. I was fully expecting some comment about the name of my ship but none came. I have often wondered what the officers on the Bridge of the Queen Elizabeth thought when I signalled 'King William'. Did they think I was some kind of wise guy? I shall never know.

I also liked to signal to warships and once had the exciting experience of making contact with the famous British aircraft carrier, the 'Ark Royal.' On another occasion during a North Atlantic crossing I attempted to talk to a submarine. At that time the Cold War was at its height and the Cuban Missile Crisis was about to take place. The submarine kept us company for several days and was never more than a mile or two away.

One dark night I called it up on the Aldis. It took quite some time to get a reply but I persisted. Eventually I asked 'What ship are you?' Their answer was 'What ship are you?' I gave them my details; they acknowledged my message and then shut down. I was quite indignant about this and called them up again. It took them quite a long time to respond and I got a very curt reply of 'Ships of the USSR do not reveal their identity or destination. Goodnight.' Pretty good English for a Russian I thought. Within minutes she was gone and we never saw her again. I assumed she imagined that we would report her position to the British Admiralty. I have to say, that prior to a voyage to Leningrad, several sinister looking men in grey suits visited the Captain. He was given a camera and asked to photograph Russian Warships and their bases.

The whole point of being proficient with the Aldis Lamp was in case we needed to send or receive an important message. I am glad to say that one day my skills were required. We were heading for New Orleans which, of course, is situated on the Mississippi River. The sky had been overcast the whole time as we crossed the Gulf of Mexico and so we had not been able to obtain any sun or star sights. We were not sure exactly where we were; we were looking for the Mississippi River Delta.

On the day we were due to make a landfall, I arrived on the Bridge at eight a.m. The ship had stopped, the weather was foggy and the Captain and the Chief Officer looked very worried. The echo sounder showed that we were in shallow water and there was a noise like the sound of breakers. The radar was switched on but because the nearest land was very flat and low-lying the information it provided was not much use.

We lay there wallowing about in the swell not daring to move. Slowly the morning sun began to burn the fog away. To our horror we began to see waves breaking over rocks about a mile away. Slowly we began to pick out the shape of a lighthouse. 'Get the Aldis Lamp out Third Mate. Call them up and ask them where we are.' To my surprise I received a prompt reply; luckily the lighthouse keeper was really on the ball. He told us exactly where we were. Our position was plotted on the chart and a course laid off. Soon it was 'Full Ahead Engines' and off we sailed to pick up the river pilot. That morning I felt a great deal of satisfaction from being able to make a reliable contribution to the safety of the crew and the ship.

In port, a Navigating Officer takes on the role of Cargo Officer. In my ten years at sea, before the advent of container ships, I served on trampships, tankers, cargo ships, cargo passenger ships and freezers.

Generally speaking, apart from tramping, we loaded manufactured goods in the U.K and took them to countries all over the world. These goods could range from dressmaker's pins to fire engines. Our deck cargoes were made up of railway carriages, locomotives and double decker buses. On one voyage we took live bulls to Cape Town. These highly prized bulls, being exported for breeding purposes lived on deck in specially constructed shelters. I was astonished that these animals stood for three weeks without moving, all the way to South Africa.

In bad weather waves would wash right over the main deck, so deck cargoes had to be securely fastened with wire lashings tightened by bottlescrews[39]. One foul night, at about two a.m., a huge wave hit a railway carriage so hard that it was left half hanging over the side. The Second Mate immediately called the Captain and briefed him about the situation. The Captain muttered only three words 'Cut it loose' and went back to sleep. The Second Mate called out some sailors who cut the remaining lashings with axes and the carriage plunged to the bottom of the sea. Luckily the bulls were better situated, protected and quite safe.

Loading manufactured goods in the U.K was easy because shore staff did all the planning. All we had to do was prevent pilfering and familiarise ourselves with the type of cargo and its destination. Eventually, when the loading was complete, we would be presented with a cargo plan and our destination or, in most cases, several destinations.

Weeks or months later, having discharged our cargo, we usually loaded raw materials which could include food. Sometimes our cargo might be ten thousand tons of iron ore, sulphur, grain or even coal dust. It is difficult to imagine what the decks, our clothes or our cabins were like when loading coal dust. Even six months after discharging a bulk cargo of sulphur dust our eyes became red and painful every time we opened the hatches.

On my very first voyage we sailed to Conakry, Guinea, West Africa. There we loaded iron ore by means of a conveyor belt. The conveyor belt was permanently fixed so we had to continually move the ship ahead and astern by heaving on the mooring ropes. We kept this up for forty-eight hours by which time we were utterly exhausted. At this point tiredness had made me careless and I trapped my finger in a steel weather door and pulled the nail off. The intense pain coupled with weariness made me want to sit down and weep, but there was no time for that. We now had to batten down the hatches[40], let go of the mooring ropes, haul them aboard and proceed to sea.

We often loaded a full cargo of grain. Loose grain behaves like a liquid, so that if the ship rolls, the grain will flow to one side; unchecked this would eventually cause the ship to capsize. To prevent such a catastrophe the Carpenter and crew constructed wooden partitions in every hatch.

Discharging a cargo of grain in Yokohama, Japan I witnessed an almost unbelievable sight. Unusually we were not moored up to a jetty, but between two buoys and, to my mind, the cargo was being discharged in a rather primitive way. Grabs were fixed to our derricks and barges surrounded the vessel. The grabs were dropped into the grain, closed up, heaved up into the air, swung across the deck and the load dropped into barges. The grabs were rather worn and the grain flowed like water through cracks. Men continually swept up the spilt grain on the deck and returned it to the hold, but some grain was lost between the ship's sides and the barges.

Watching this process, I suddenly became aware of small open boats pumping air to hard hat divers on the seabed surrounding the ship. I was very curious as to what they were doing and eventually asked a Japanese foreman. I was astounded to find out that they were scraping up the grain that had fallen to the seabed. Every time a sack was full it was hauled up and an empty one sent down. 'But it wouldn't be fit for human consumption,' I protested, 'No,' I was told, 'but it would be fit for animals.'

Another remarkable fact was that, as the grain was being discharged, a group of dockworkers did nothing but sweep down the holds. By the time we were empty, there was absolutely no grain left as they had even removed rubbish from previous cargoes, thus saving the crew many days of work cleaning out the holds themselves. This hard work, attention to detail, and abhorrence of waste must surely be one of the factors that has made Japan one of the most wealthy and successful nations on Earth.

Whilst it was a pleasure to visit some countries the same could not be said of others. We had worked our way down the Brazilian coast and were due to visit Montevideo in Uruguay and Buenos Aires in Argentina. The Rio de la Plata turned out to be a shallow muddy river but at least I saw the site of the famous 'Battle of the River Plate.' We grounded several times whilst trying to make port, slithering across the mud. The pilot didn't seem to be the slightest bit concerned and told us it was quite normal.

We were visiting Buenos Aires to load large quantities of tinned meat, including the famous corned beef. The ship's agent briefed the Captain on some local regulations. We must not let the courtesy Argentinian flag touch the deck when hoisting it every morning at eight a.m. This was considered an insult and the offender was likely to be locked up for twenty-four hours. The other issue was rats. The vessel must make sure that every mooring rope was fitted with a rat guard and that the gangway was painted brilliant white. It was believed that rats on the ship would not cross a white area to get ashore. If these regulations were not observed the ship was liable to be fined the equivalent of five hundred pounds.

As you can imagine the Third Mate and the apprentices had no wish to insult the Argentineans but were even more concerned about being locked up for twenty-four hours. The eight 'o' clock event of hoisting the flags became quite a ceremony, with everybody clutching at the wretched flag to make sure it didn't inadvertently touch the deck. We noted that we were being closely observed.

They did have a rat problem in Buenos Aires, probably related to the vast quantities of meat exported from there. We were actually rat free and the Argentineans would have been better advised not to insist on rat guards. In that way, we would have probably taken some of their rats away with us.

Unfortunately as the ship surged about, the rat guards, round pieces of metal about the size of a dustbin lid, tended to fall off. The Captain had us checking them every hour, twenty-four hours a day. In addition, we freshly painted the gangway pure white but it was frequently muddied by the constant tramp of feet. The authorities continually complained and we obligingly repainted it every twenty-four hours. This proved an interminable task as the paint never managed to dry properly.

For some strange reason we were asked to shift ship to another dock every day. This of course was very hard work and time consuming. We became heartily sick of this daily ritual. Whether they resented the flag we flew above the stern or extremely bad organisation on their part, we never managed to find out.

Going ashore was very interesting and enjoyable, but we encountered another common problem. All over the world taxi drivers, bars and traders would attempt to overcharge sailors because of their lack of local knowledge. The Argentineans were quite unique. Even having caught them out once, they would unashamedly try over and over again to relieve us of our hard- earned cash. They did, however, have a very effective way of dealing with drunken or disruptive sailors. If arrested, the culprits would be locked up for the night and the next day made to sweep the streets.

Walking back to the ship after having a night out was something of a nightmare. Again, probably related to the proximity of meat, numerous packs of half-wild dogs roamed the docks. I was never at ease with dogs and being surrounded by a pack of about twenty hungry looking, unkempt brutes alarmed me. I felt that if I fell down the worse for drink, or if I tripped over a railway line, I would be their next meal. Not only was it a relief to get back on-board, it was a great relief to set sail for pastures new.

For me the greatest thrill was to load a cargo in an under developed country, a country that was not westernised with a culture very different to our own. Approaching the entrance to the West African Creeks, a number of pilots arrived together by canoe. A lively squabble took place as to who was going to be our pilot. The Captain had already been advised on whom to employ, so we allowed Wilson Goola to come on-board and he turned out to be an excellent choice. Sailing far up the creeks was a uniquely memorable experience; the ship simply sailed through luxuriant jungle with numerous colourful birds and chattering monkeys swinging about in the trees. Sometimes the river was so narrow that branches were chafing along the ship's sides. Insects of all kinds rained down on deck with one particularly fierce specimen, about the size of a fist, which croaked like a frog when it was squeezed.

We passed primitive villages that would have looked the same two thousand years ago, just mud huts on a river bank. Some of the older sailors had been saving up tins and bottles which they began to accumulate on the deck. When I asked what for, I was furtively told, 'You'll see.'

One night we anchored in a lake within sight of village fires which burned brightly in the distance. The local girls, usually topless, quickly came out close to our ship in their canoes. Now I found out what the tins and bottles were for. The girls kept shouting a word like 'Dashmio', which meant 'Give me something.' In response the sailors enthusiastically persuaded them to perform a striptease in exchange for the containers. A number of the sailors were keen to go ashore with the very willing girls but Wilson Goola strongly advised against it. He told them 'If you go ashore with those girls, we shall probably never see you again.' Wisely, they took heed of his advice.

Wilson Goola went for a daily swim and I reasoned that if it was safe enough for him, it was safe enough for me. Someone claimed that they had seen a baby crocodile about eighteen inches long swimming around the ship. I made enquiries and Wilson Goola told me that in the early nineteen hundreds, the Captains of ships had amused themselves by blasting away at crocodiles with hunting rifles. The result of this was that the crocodiles had retreated up the quieter, shallower and undisturbed creeks.

We visited Burutu, Warri, and Sapele in Nigeria to load hardwood logs for the U.K. There were no jetties, so we simply moored up to the trees and the logs were floated to the ship's side. The loading of the logs was extremely dangerous and required a great deal of skill. A local workforce, who all had the most marvellous physiques, carried this out. Having got a log safely into the hold it then had to be moved to one side or the other. The logs, weighing ten to fifteen tons, were wet and slimy having just been lifted out of the water. Sometimes the logs would suddenly start sliding and the labourers had to jump for their lives. Being struck by one of these logs would have meant instant death.

In the course of this there was great excitement as a huge snake fell off a log when it was being lifted out of the water. This immediately initiated a hunt and all work stopped whilst the men pursued this dangerous creature. First it swam through the water followed by the men jumping from log to log. It reached the riverbank and attempted to escape through the bushes. Still with men in hot pursuit it made the mistake of climbing up a tree. Spears seemed to appear as if by magic. I had a ringside seat high up on the ship and witnessed the great glee and excitement when the poor creature was killed. I suppose that from the Nigerians point of view they had killed a poisonous reptile, which had strayed into an area where they worked and lived. For my part, I didn't risk swimming in those waters again.

It was the custom for the ship's agent to give the Captain a gift. One day we were all sitting in the Saloon having dinner when the agent walked in and announced that he had brought the Captain a gift. Sitting in the Saloon was the Chief Engineer's wife who had joined him for the trip. She was a very serious Welsh lady, far from broad-minded who normally attended chapel every Sunday. The Captain naturally wanted to see his gift, so the agent called in a very curvaceous girl of about fourteen. The Captain was a very respectable, married, and tea-total man. He had no interest in the girl but had noticed the shocked and disapproving look that appeared on the Chief's wife's face. With a mischievous look on his face he shouted 'Steward, take this girl up to my cabin. Give her a scrub in a hot bath. I'll be up in ten minutes.' The Chief's wife was completely taken in and remained stony faced for the rest of the meal whilst the rest of us were nearly choking, red-faced and trying not to laugh. Evidently it took the Chief several days to convince his wife that it was all a practical joke.

The Chief's wife also had another startling experience in Ghana. We had anchored during the night at an open roadstead port[41] called Accra and she had decided to have a breath of fresh air before going for breakfast. I just happened to be on hand when she stepped outside of her accommodation. She was utterly shocked to find herself surrounded by naked, superbly muscular, black men who were exceptionally well endowed in every department. She retreated rapidly but made two more attempts to come outside. I felt sure that her embarrassment had turned to curiosity and then to admiration.

What I was going to see for the first time was also in some ways startling but perhaps fascinating would be a more appropriate word. There was no harbour for large vessels so our general cargo had to be discharged using our own derricks, into what might be called large canoes. The canoes were propelled by paddles and, if I remember correctly, one steering oar. The men in the boats did not seem to own a single item of clothing and all seemed to be supreme physical specimens.

Dropping a sling or tray of cargo into the bottom of the canoe was quite hazardous. If it were off centre, the canoe would list over and quite rapidly start taking in seawater. Then there would be much excited shouting, the sling would be lifted and another attempt made.

Before paddling furiously for the shore, a 'chitty' was needed to prove the number of journeys made because payment was by results. One of the paddlers had to come aboard to collect their note. A rope was provided at each hatch for these men to climb up: it was not necessary to provide a ladder. Once the cargo was safely in the canoe they were off. As soon as the man on board the ship got his chitty, he put it in his mouth, dived overboard and swam after the canoe.

Once loaded the canoes had very little freeboard[42] and faced a dangerous journey of about one-mile. During our stay in Accra I saw several canoes sink in choppy weather. The crews would hold on to their paddles and stay in a close group and wait for someone to pick them up. The only problem was that the other crews were so busy earning money that no one was very keen to do so. I timed one group of men floating around for about two hours before being rescued. No one seemed to be the slightest bit concerned about the presence of sharks and barracudas. Evidently the seabed was littered with sunken canoes containing every conceivable cargo including brand new, now ruined, cars.

46

Loading one cargo of, say, iron ore at a foreign port destined for the U.K. was easy. Imagine loading rice, tea, cotton, rubber, jute, nuts, silk, carpets and pepper at six ports on the Indian coast for London, Bristol, Liverpool, Manchester and Glasgow. The cargoes have to be loaded so that: a) the ship remains on an even keel, b) the ship is not listing to port or starboard, c) the cargoes are not able to contaminate each other and d) the consignments are accessible at each port. If, in error, five hundred tons of rice to be discharged in London, was buried under three hundred tons of cotton for Glasgow then the Chief Officer would have probably faced dismissal.

It was usually my job to maintain a master plan of where every item of cargo was stored, how much there was of it and where it was to be discharged. As the last sling of cargo was loaded, my master plan had to be completed and handed to the ship's agent. It was then flown to the U.K and copied. The copies were then forwarded to all the interested parties in the receiving ports. My head would be on the block if, say, for example, a hundred tons of silk for Liverpool was not where it should be and could not be found.

CHAPTER 4

Pilfering Knitting Needles

I was watching as a gang of dockers loaded a tray of cartons which was swinging wildly about in the air. As it was lowered into the hold one of the cartons hit the hatch coaming[43] and I heard the unmistakable tinkle of broken glass. The tray was hoisted up again and halted about seven feet above the deck. Soon a clear, brown liquid was trickling out of the corner of the carton. The dockers, assembling beneath the carton, took it in turns to open their mouths and let the fluid trickle in whilst others caught the fluid in tin mugs and shared it with those working down in the hold. I looked at the carton, puzzled as to what they were drinking. On its side was marked 'Scotch Whisky'. I was aghast, thinking they would surely swallow pieces of broken glass, but then realised that the carton and its packing acted as a filter. The tray hitting the hatch coaming had not been an accident but had been carried out very skilfully. This was my first experience of the world-wide problem of pilfering.

The Dock Police, ship's crews, security men and night watchmen carried out a never-ending war to prevent theft. Not only was the ship's cargo at risk, but any of the ship's equipment that could be lifted or lowered into a waiting small boat.

Once in port security measures had to be put in place. Cabin doors had to be locked and portholes clamped down. One Chief Officer's wife, whom we had nicknamed the Duchess because of her grandiose disposition, managed to slam down a heavy brass porthole on the fingers of a would be thief. His arm had been exploring the inside of her cabin and, judging by the howl of pain, justice had been meted out. Nothing more was seen of him.

As a young boy, I was puzzled when I saw Birkenhead dockers drinking out of beautiful bone china teacups. One Saturday dinnertime, I noticed a docker going home wearing several expensive looking jumpers. It was much later that I realised how these items had been sourced.

Some ships were provided with a huge steel locker, into which valuable cargoes could be stowed. Brian, the other apprentice and I had to take turns in this locker to prevent theft. It was a very unpleasant and boring job just sitting there watching the dockers. They hated our presence and would still try to break into boxes when out of our line of vision. Occasionally, we would see a policeman peering down into the hatch, which gave us some comfort. I often felt that if it were not for the police, the dockers would cut our throats or throw us down the hold.

Brian had an unfortunate experience whilst he was on locker duty. A docker, in a very friendly fashion, asked him if he fancied a bottle of beer. Brian eagerly said yes and innocently began drinking from the proffered bottle. He was completely unaware that the docker had stolen the beer out of the cargo until suddenly, all around him, the dockers began opening other bottles. In a panic, Brian tried to stop them, but they just laughed and reminded him 'You started it first mate'. Brian fled, red faced, and fetched the Chief Officer. Of course, there was nothing to be seen when he arrived. Following that embarrassing experience Brian was excused further locker duty.

Most pilfering went on unseen; the only evidence was the remaining litter of empty cartons, bottles and tins. Once, after discharging a cargo of tinned fruit, I found hundreds of tins strewn about the holds. Closer inspection of their contents revealed a mass of rotting pineapple. Each tin had two small holes in the top made by a docker's cargo hook so that the juice could be consumed and the tin discarded. The waste appalled me and I couldn't understand how so much juice had been drunk.

General cargo was packed into cartons and wooden boxes. The boxes could be as big as a garden shed or a room in a house. In Capetown, a hatch foreman drew our attention to a discovery he had made down in one of the holds. During loading in Liverpool the dockers had constructed a secret room amongst the cargo. The compartment had a floor, four walls and a ceiling. Lighting had been provided by one of the ship's clusters[44]. Smaller boxes had been used for chairs and a table. The secret space was littered with empty beer and spirit bottles, and a pack of playing cards still lay on the makeshift table. How long their party and card games had gone on whilst we were blissfully unaware, nobody knew.

Some pilfering was born of desperate poverty. We regularly visited Beira and Lourenco Marques (Maputo) in Mozambique, which at that time was a Portugese colony. The Africans who worked on the docks were barefoot, dressed in rags and obviously very poor. One night two menacing looking Portuguese security men dragged a very unhappy looking dockworker up to me. He was wearing a magnificent pair of new, brown leather shoes which the security men were certain he had stolen out of the cargo. They asked me to check the cargo manifest because they were unable to find any cartons that had been broken into. I went to the ship's office, checked our lists and returned to tell them that we were not carrying any shoes. The African, who had probably stolen the shoes from another ship, said something gleefully, to the effect of, 'There I told you so.' This enraged the two Portuguese security guards who promptly began to flog him with a two and a half-inch manilla rope, something I was not prepared to tolerate. This was a British ship and while I was not against appropriate punishment I considered lashing a man with a rope to be barbaric. I ordered the two Portuguese men off the ship. Unfortunately this did not have the desired effect as they became beside themselves with rage. They dragged the poor African with them as they left the ship. Once on the quayside they gave him a terrible beating with fists and feet. Sadly I could no longer help him and I was further dismayed to see them take his work permit with them. This was serious as it meant he would not be able to work on the docks again. Although the world can be a cruel place I did notice that he walked away with his very smart shoes.

In Beira I witnessed a theft that was as truly remarkable as seeing the divers on the seabed in Japan. We were discharging cargo twenty-four hours a day and I was on night-work. One of my duties was to continually visit the hatches to prevent pilfering. The holds were illuminated with the ship's clusters. This meant that the hold was well lit where the dockers were actually working whilst other areas of the hold were in near darkness. I was able to venture into these dark areas without anyone seeing me.

In African countries, with a clear sky, the temperature can plummet at night. The scantily dressed, almost destitute Africans were suffering with the cold. Prowling about down one of the holds I noticed a man behaving very strangely. He was in a dark corner and his arms were continually jerking about. I crept closer and the man was so engrossed in his activity that he never saw me. As my eyes became accustomed to the dark I was astonished to see that he was knitting. It appeared that he had broken open some cartons and found some bicycle spokes in one and wool in another. At that stage he had only completed a few square inches. I crept away, fascinated, wondering what he could be knitting.

During the long night I visited the man several times, making sure that he never saw me come or go. He continued knitting all night and the garment began to take some shape. I was truly impressed to see that his knitting had a pattern to it. But what was I to do with his poverty, the cold, and his ingenuity? Should I apprehend him?

To my surprise and unashamed delight the man went home the following morning wearing a very smart grey jumper. There is a saying that 'Necessity is the mother of invention'. Surely this was a prime example of that. I chose to overlook his theft.

I arrived on the Bridge at eight p.m. for the First Watch. We were at anchor in Port Tewfik, Egypt, waiting to join a convoy to sail through the Suez Canal. It was a beautiful, peaceful evening and I looked forward to an easy watch. The Chief Officer was a very smart man, well educated but perhaps a little officious. He handed over to me and then said something very puzzling. 'You'll see a lot of activity on the foredeck. Just ignore it, it's nothing to do with you.' We were not working cargo so I asked a few questions but he refused to elaborate. About nine p.m. a large number of Egyptians arrived in small boats and boarded the ship. My doubts vanished when I suddenly realised that the Chief Officer was about to sell some of the ship's stores and equipment. I was very worried as the Captain always came onto the Bridge at ten 'o' clock for a cup of tea. What could I do? Nothing, I decided; best to mind my own business.

Bang on ten 'o' clock the Old Man walked through the chartroom door and strolled towards the wheelhouse windows. By now the foredeck was alive with the activity of men lowering goods into the waiting boats. The Captain reached a window and as he was taking in the scene his body stiffened and he shouted 'My God Third Mate! What's going on down there?' As calmly as I could, I said, 'Rope, canvas, wire and paint going over the side into the boats' By now he was apoplectic, 'Well why haven't you stopped it?' he spluttered. I didn't want to name names and run the risk of the rest of the voyage being unpleasant. Choosing my words carefully I said, 'An officer more senior than myself has told me not to interfere.' The Captain understood the message very quickly, as, in the chain of command between him and me remained only the Second Officer and Chief Officer. He hurriedly left the Bridge without a word. A few moments later I saw the amusing spectacle of the Chief Officer running up the foredeck in his pyjamas. It took him some considerable time to restore order and to placate a group of angry Egyptians who were less than happy that their lucrative night's work was being curtailed. No one mentioned the incident again and I was left wondering why a man on a good salary, soon to be ship's Master himself, would risk his career for a few pounds in his back pocket. Sometimes I feel that the more we earn, the greedier we get.

A mooring rope, even nearly worn out, is a very valuable item. In port there are six or eight of them just lying on the deck. We were in Aden, moored up to buoys and bunkering. Once again I had drawn the short straw and was on night duty. All I had to do was walk around the deck every hour or so, check the moorings and make sure that no unauthorised persons had boarded the ship. It was going to be a long, tedious night and I knew that by three in the morning I would be struggling to stay awake. We had a full deck cargo of forty-gallon drums, so to walk about on top of them needed some care.

By the early hours of the morning everyone was asleep except for one engineer who was sweating down in the engine room. Apart from the noise of the generator the ship was silent and peaceful. For some reason I was wearing a full tropical uniform, including a hat, which was unusual for me. I decided to have a stroll round the stern of the ship. I was ambling along, whistling quietly though my mind was far away. As I came round the corner of the poop I was jolted into full concentration. A couple of yards in front of me were two rather fat Arabs, feeding a mooring rope over the side into a small rowing boat. The two men were as startled as I was. In retrospect I feel sure that had I not been wearing a smart uniform I might soon have been laid on my back with a knife between my ribs. As it was, these two took to their heels with me in hot pursuit. The Arabs were not very good at running across the tops of the drums and I began to gain on them. At that point I began to wonder what I would do if I caught them. The solution, much safer for me, was not to catch them, so I slowed down and made as much noise as possible. This had the desired effect for, instead of turning to fight, the two rogues jumped over the side. They started swimming to shore and I decided to help them on their way. I was now standing outside the galley, so I ran in and collected an armful of coal. Rushing to the ship's side I hurled pieces of coal at their fleeing forms. Judging by the howls of pain and gurgled curses I must have scored some direct hits. It now occurred to me that the rowing boat might be able to get away with our mooring rope. I ran back but the boat was gone, and our rope was left hanging over the side. I set a winch going, put the rope on the drum end and hauled it back on-board. All this drama had gone on without another person on the ship knowing anything about it. I was feeling rather pleased with myself even though my hands, arms, and once white shirt were black with coal dust. Looking back I have often wondered what would have happened if I had not been wearing a uniform. The outcome might have been very different.

Living in Britain with its well developed institutions of law and order, it is easy to believe that all countries are law-abiding, civilised places. When we hear of pirates, equipped with fast motorboats and modern weapons, we are reminded that some parts of the world can be very dangerous indeed. I heard of a British tanker that ran aground on the wild and remote coast of Yemen. The crew were attacked by tribesmen but managed to hold them at bay with very hot water hoses normally used for cleaning the oil tanks. This attack continued until the crew managed to get the ship re-floated.

During my years at sea we all thought that pirates were a thing of the past, but I was involved in an alarming experience in India whilst we were loading tea in Pondicherry on the south east coast. One day the police visited the Captain and told him that the ship was going to be attacked that night by 'dacoits.' 'Dacoits,' we thought, 'what the hell are dacoits?' A dacoit, we soon discovered, is a member of an Indian armed gang.

The Captain was not particularly perturbed as he thought the police would be present and able to protect us. Unfortunately, the police had other ideas, claiming that they were undermanned and over stretched. We would have to organise our own defence. The pattern of previous attacks was that the men would swim to the ship's side. Dacoits would infiltrate the bona fide dock workers and throw chests of tea overboard to the men in the water. The stakes were high because one tea chest was the equivalent to one man's wages for a year. No guns were expected but it was thought the robbers on board would be armed with knives.

The Captain called a meeting in the saloon to discuss defence tactics. The best we could come up with was to arm ourselves with sledgehammer and axe handles. We also stockpiled heaps of missiles to throw at any men in the water.

When darkness fell we hid ourselves along the off shore side of the ship. I must say that I did not really believe that anyone would come so I was very surprised when a number of heads appeared amid the inky gloom, silently moving through the water. The atmosphere on the ship was electric. A number of the dockworkers on the ship seemed to be eyeing us malevolently. Would they make a move? We waited until the men in the water were very close to the ship's side. They appeared to be using some kind of float for support. Trying to watch the men on the ship, we pelted the dacoits in the water until our ammunition was exhausted. They immediately began to swim away as fast as they could, some suffering painful direct hits. None of their crooked associates on board moved or displayed any signs of being in league with them. That was the end of the matter; the police intelligence had been accurate even though they were not prepared to help us.

The last of my experiences in this chapter recounts some questionable activities that took place on a ship we were ordered to take to a scrapyard. Built in 1929, it was now thirty years old. On its maiden voyage people flocked to see it because it was years ahead of its time. It had a diesel engine, all electric winches and electric heating in the cabins. Even in 1959 it still looked modern compared with many contemporary vessels. Its weakness was the metal it was made of. Jagged holes were appearing in tanks and bulkheads, making the cost of repairs uneconomical. The heating in the accommodation area was failing and in high latitudes it was a struggle to keep warm. In Portland, Maine, North America, the temperature dropped to minus thirty at night. I vividly remember waking up one morning to find my sheets frozen to the wooden bulkhead and ice on the inside of my porthole. The intense cold that night did some damage to my elbows, the consequences of which lasted for years.

We received orders to proceed to Cronulla, Australia, to load ten thousand tons of grain, then on to Yokohama and, once discharged, hand the ship over to the breakers. It occurred to the Chief Officer, Second Engineer and Bosun that the new owners would not have an inventory of the stores and equipment aboard the ship, nor were we asked to compile one. It also seemed sensible to assume that the new owners would not expect a ship going to be broken up to arrive with a surplus of stores and equipment. In fact, the ship was liberally equipped and the expendable stores were almost untouched.

Cronulla turned out to be a small port with a very friendly population. As a crew, however, we met with a potential disaster of great magnitude - we would not be allowed in the bars or hotels unless accompanied by a lady. There were no women on board so we had no option but to resort to pleading with perfect strangers. Women from sixteen to ninety were propositioned in the street in an attempt to assuage our parched throats. No one seemed to mind though as, accompanied by a motley assortment of women, we drank our fill of the beer sold to us by grateful landlords and hotel owners.

Following these memorable nights in the town, it was not very long before everyone in Cronulla knew that we were taking the ship to Japan to be scrapped. At that time the Second World War was still fresh in everyone's minds. A nurse who had been a prisoner of war in Japan lived in the town; her treatment at the hands of the Japanese had been particularly horrific.

As a result the local Australians had strong views on what we should, and should not, take to the Land of the Rising Sun.

Every evening, at the end of cargo work, a line of cars, cars with trailers and vans arrived at the bottom of the gangway. Negotiations would then begin to purchase, very cheaply, a great variety of goods. If the Captain was aware of what was going on then he kept a low profile. The Australians managed to find tools and equipment that we never knew we had. I remember having a beer with the First Mate one night when a chap came to his open cabin door and said 'I'll give you twenty quid for the anvil that's in the tweendeck'.

'Done' said the Mate and he chuckled as the delighted man left.

'What are you laughing at?' I asked as the man went to struggle with his purchase.

'Well,' said the Mate, 'I just made twenty quid and I didn't even know we had an anvil on board the ship.' How the man managed to carry the anvil ashore remains a mystery.

With all the paint, wood and brushes the Australians had acquired, the town became a hive of activity. Houses were being painted, fences and gates constructed. The noise of hammering was everywhere. What with our drinking and business antics, we had made many friends. The day arrived when our grain cargo was fully loaded. We slipped our moorings one sunny afternoon and set course for Japan. Leaving port we had to sail parallel to a headland for a few miles. To our surprise the townspeople drove along the headland waving and blowing their car horns until we were out of sight. It was a very sad farewell to friends we would never see again.

Chapter 5

Old Seadogs and Eccentrics

On my second voyage I met a fascinating Able Seaman called Fred. He was sixty-eight and I reckoned he must have been born in 1887. Fred was about five feet four inches tall and walked with a creak. His proud boast was that he only had 'one leg, one kidney and one ball'. The creaking walk was caused by a rather primitive artificial leg, which did not seem to trouble him in the slightest. He had served in the Merchant Navy through two World Wars, torpedoed three times and on one of those occasions had lost his leg and a testicle. How he lost his kidney I never found out. I learnt not to probe too deeply into people's wartime experiences having once asked a Chief Steward about the obvious burn scars on his face. It was only when someone kicked me under the table that I saw tears rolling down his face. After that, I just listened to what people were prepared to tell me.

Fred told me that his first trip to sea had been on a sailing ship when he was fourteen. All went well until it was time to set sail. The First Mate, often the toughest man on the ship, shouted an order to the sailors about breaking out the sails which was totally incomprehensible to Fred. The Sailors ran off, leaving him standing there not knowing what to do. With that the Mate ran up and hit him hard with a belaying pin[45] which knocked poor Fred down. From then on, if the Mate shouted an order, he just ran off with the other Sailors, even if he didn't have a clue about what to do.

Fred always had a smile on his coppery, weather beaten face. Regardless of the climate he wore a knitted skullcap and his rugged face seemed as though it had been chiselled out of granite. Working with Fred was a joy. He was always cheerful and had an endless stream of smutty jokes for those who chose to listen. He would not climb the mast, go down the hold or work over the side on a stage. Apart from that he was more than capable of every job on the deck. Nobody seemed to be the slightest bit concerned about his handicap.

On one occasion we were cleaning rubbish out of the hatches. Fred and I were working on deck, pulling up the debris with a rope and bucket and throwing it over the side. All the while Fred was regaling me with his repertoire of jokes. Unfortunately, I laughed so much that I let go of the heavy bucket, which shot through the hatch, accelerating as it did so. Down in the bottom of the hold was Mr. Jones the Bosun and several sailors. Luckily, the Bosun always wore a black beret, which I think saved him from serious injury. The galvanised bucket, with a conical underside, hit him square on the head. If the edge of the bucket had struck him he would undoubtedly have suffered a fractured skull.

Mr. Jones was, beneath his tough veneer, a kindly man but not too happy about being hit on the head with a bucket, to say the least. A stream of foul language and abuse floated up from forty feet below. When I dared to peep over the hatch coaming I saw the Bosun's upturned face. He was holding his beret in his hand, wreathed in a cloud of dust. The sight of my face prompted a further tirade of swearing and invective. Of course, Fred, the cause of the incident, was helpless with laughter and pretending innocence.

Happily, the Bosun was not a man to bear a grudge. I was dreading him coming up out of the hatch later that morning. By way of retribution I thought he would have me cleaning out the bilges or performing some equally obnoxious task. When he did eventually come up, he seemed to have forgotten all about the incident, perhaps assuming it had been a pure accident.

Fred was a ladies man. No sooner was the gangway down in a new port than he was hop legging it up the road. In a very short space of time he would have a very pretty young lady on his arm. This had the effect of making him smile even more broadly than usual. How a man of his years managed to attract women a third of his age I will never know. This indeed was the legendary sailor with 'a girl in every port'!

We subsequently discovered that, despite his bachelor image, he was married with six children. When we visited Hull, his home port, we thought it strange that he did not want shore leave. We soon found out the reason for this when his wife came aboard looking for him. Well before his arrival in Hull, the old rogue had spent all his wages.

Some seemingly smart and efficient men are not always likeable. Mr. Thorner was a faultless Chief Officer but not the most pleasant of colleagues. We were both serving on a small passenger cargo ship trading between Pakistan, India and the U.K. which Mr. Thorner always did his best to keep spick and span. The outside paintwork was washed regularly and the decks scrubbed daily.

Sometimes passengers returning to the U.K. following a spell of living and working abroad had a dog with them, and a ship is no place for a dog. I saw one dog killed when it fell down a hold. At sea it was used to running around the decks and jumping onto the hatch covers. In port, the hatch covers were removed to allow the cargo to be discharged. No one realised that at deck level, the poor animal was unable see that the hatches were open. He made his usual jump and fell to the metal deck far below. It did not fall to its death but was so badly injured that, unfortunately, it had to be destroyed.

There was one particular dog that Mr. Thorner hated with a passion. The reason for his dislike of the dog was because each day it left its calling card and nobody was inclined to remove the offending mess. Whether he had treated the dog badly, or perhaps given it a kick when nobody was looking, I had no way of knowing. I believe, however, that the dog knew it had an enemy in the Chief Officer. Over the years since I have come to believe that an animal, particularly a dog, is well capable off planning and carrying out a vengeful act if it is treated badly by another animal or human being.

One day, when the Chief Officer was on watch, the dog must have decided to strike. It entered our accommodation, where it had never been before, and found Mr. Thorner's cabin. It jumped onto his double bed, pulled all the bedclothes into a pyramid and copiously defecated upon them. Nobody saw it come or go. One can only imagine the Chief's reaction when he came down, exhausted after four hours on the Bridge. In a fit of rage, he swept up the mattress, sheets, pillows and counterpane and threw the lot into the sea. There was nothing he could do about it though, since the dog belonged to a valued and respected passenger. The incident gave some amusement and concealed pleasure to those of us who didn't care for Mr. Thorner all that much.

In Chittagong, Pakistan, we often found ourselves moored up with several other ships of the same company. We knew the crews and ships because we had worked on them ourselves; this often led to drunken parties as we renewed old acquaintances. One of these ships had a somewhat unconventional Chief Officer called Mr. Cutter. His party piece, when sufficiently lubricated, was to bite off someone's tie. The bite was about three inches below the knot and was helped by pulling hard on the loose ends. I'd heard about this strange practise but didn't really believe it until I saw Mr. Thorner's tie bitten into three pieces. Mr. Thorner, on the other hand, failed to see the funny side of this and, like the dog, was secretly planning his revenge.

One afternoon, he said to me, 'John, find a pair of scissors and a screwdriver. We have a little job to do.' Knowing that Cutter was ashore, we set off on our clandestine mission. Unchallenged, as the Captain was unaware of our presence, we easily boarded his ship as it lay unguarded at the dockside. Mr. Thorner still had a key to Mr. Cutter's cabin from the time when he had worked on the ship. I was told to unscrew the hinges on the cabin door whilst the Chief found all of Mr. Cutter's ties. He had a fine collection of expensive ties, and I counted seventeen in all. Mr. Thorner duly cut them up with the scissors and then tied them all up in a long line. He then hung the line up around the cabin like a gaudy Christmas streamer. We then carefully put the door back into place as if it was shut and locked.

Evidently, Mr. Cutter returned later in the day, and after putting his key in the lock, was startled as the door fell with a crash to the floor. Gazing beyond the frame he was utterly astonished to find his precious ties festooned in tatters around the cabin. No one was the slightest bit sympathetic; in fact, most of the sailors were delighted with this payback for their own savaged neckwear. After this brutal, but rather sweet revenge, no one heard of him ever biting off a tie again.

There is a saying that life at sea will turn a man to religion or drink. In my experience, it was almost always the latter. Mr. Matthews, another Chief Officer, was the exception to the rule. He was a non-swearing, teetotal, practising Christian. He was also a fine seaman. Every Sunday morning he used to invite us to a service in his cabin. We always politely declined but were in receipt of one whether we liked it or not. He had numerous services on tape, complete with hymns and prayers, which he played loudly with his cabin door wide open. He was convinced that someone up above was looking out for him and sometimes events seemed to indicate he may well have been right.

One remarkable incident occurred when we were serving on a heavy lift ship. The vessel had a derrick, which could lift one hundred tons. In Liverpool we were putting an extremely heavy piece of machinery into number three hatch. The heavy lift derrick was rigged with steam guys. The steam guys carefully controlled the movement of the derrick as it swung from the quayside to the centre of the hatch. A steam guy is made up of a strong wire fastened to the top of the derrick, and the wire is then led to a heavy metal block[46] fastened to an eyebolt on the deck and then to a winch. Hauling on one guy and slacking off on the other causes the derrick to swing with its heavy load.

Mr. Matthews and I were on duty keeping an eye on the proceedings. One of the steam guys was making the kind of cracking noise that we knew indicated it was under considerable strain. Suddenly, without any warning, the welding fastening the eyebolt to the deck gave way. Working like a gigantic catapult, the heavy block shot through the air and hit Mr. Matthews in the stomach. The impact threw him violently to the deck. I immediately had dreadful thoughts of serious internal injuries and rushed across to him, but was astonished when he shakily began to pick himself up. He kept telling me that he was all right, but I didn't believe him. I insisted that he go to his cabin with two of us supporting him. I still felt that he might develop grave symptoms. Returning to the deck, we nervously identified another convenient eyebolt and continued with our loading.

About ten minutes later I was flabbergasted to see the Chief coming back onto the deck. He was completely recovered and subsequently suffered no ill effects. Although not a believer in miracles or divine intervention, I could not understand how he had not been seriously injured. I was also witness to another strange incident which demonstrated that if God did exist, then He did indeed work in mysterious ways.

We were at sea, inching along the English Channel in the thickest of fog. There were many other ships in the vicinity and their fog signals were moaning sorrowfully. Mr. Matthews and I were not on duty, but standing at the rails peering hard into the cotton wool seascape. We knew that there was another ship very close to us and we were quite worried. Suddenly the fog lifted and there, only a few yards away, was a huge North Sea Ferry. Mr. Matthews started waving frantically to a couple we could see standing at the rail of the other ship. They waved excitedly back and then the fog dropped down again like a curtain. The Chief was still energetically waving and shouting. I stared at him rather strangely; 'Do you know those people?' I asked.

'Yes,' he replied, 'that was my Mum and Dad.'

I was wide-eyed and speechless. How do you explain a coincidence like that? He later discovered that they were on holiday and on their way to the Continent.

Things did not always work in his favour, however. Crossing the Indian Ocean, he found out that one of his Christian friends was passing close by. Being the Chief Officer, he was able to speak to his friend through the Wireless Operator using telegraphy. The rather tough, cynical Sparks[47] was not too happy about this but had little say in the matter. Nor were the rest of us very happy either because the transmission noise was blasting through our private radios. The conversation between the two was coming to an end with numerous biblical quotes. Right in the middle of this religious orgy the wireless equipment broke down. Mr. Matthews was quite upset and was protesting loudly. Sparks, now thoroughly browned off, retorted tersely, 'Don't worry; get your friend to walk across the water to talk to you.'

The average merchant seaman is a hardworking decent chap but there are exceptions. A few of us joined a trampship in Fowey, Cornwall to load china clay - the fine white powder essential to the manufacture of embossed wallpaper and porcelain. Each night a group of us would go ashore to visit a pub or cinema. One member of the group was an electrician called Evan Jones and I soon began to form a negative opinion of him. At about eleven 'o' clock each night, we had to return to the ship by way of a small motorboat. By this time Evan was well fuelled with drink and in quite an aggressive mood. He told us several times that he had killed a man in a fight, an admission intended to be both frightening and impressive. We were nonplussed.

From the outset it was clear that Evan was capable of strange and sometimes bizarre behaviour. One night we all went to a dance, a small affair, very much like a village hall get-together. Evan seemed to be enjoying himself immensely. During the interval he stood in the middle of the deserted dance floor and began to conduct the background music. People began to watch his antics with interest, including the girl I was chatting to. When he removed his jacket I thought he must be getting warm, but then his tie came off, and then he dropped his braces off his shoulders. At this point I began to get a bit concerned. I had a fair idea of what was going to happen next. In an instant, he pulled his trousers down and exposed himself. Two doormen rushed forward, grabbed his trousers and pulled them up again. There now started quite a struggle as Evan was determined to have his trousers down and the doormen were equally determined to keep them up. A hush had fallen over the whole dance hall and people stared as Evan was wrestled to the entrance and thrown out.

I noticed that the girl I was trying to date was slowly inching away. 'What's the matter?' I asked her.

'Is he with you?' she enquired.

'No love, never seen him before in my life' I replied. But it was no use: she had seen me coming in with him.

Within weeks the crew became very wary of Evan and he did not have a single friend aboard the ship. Nevertheless he remained an irrepressible character. Wherever we docked Evan was usually the first ashore and we began to notice that, within forty-eight hours, he had his trademark graffiti in the toilet of every seedy bar in town. What was more, he seemed to form close relationships with women of most unusual appearance. They often wore the most outlandish, colourful clothes, and seemed to have stubble on their faces and hair on their legs. Evan's preference, apparently, was for cross-dressers and transvestites.

When we were at sea he caused trouble. At mealtimes he enjoyed being deliberately provocative, hoping to encourage a heated argument. His speciality was the allegedly differing characteristics of the Scots, English, Welsh and Irish. However, as the crew realised what his intention was, Evan rapidly became the target for their regular, scornful, verbal onslaughts.

One morning I was spectator to an unusual and amusing incident. I was on watch and so I had a clear view of the foredeck. About 9:30 Evan, also known as Lecky, appeared on deck to carry out maintenance work on the electric winches. Even from high up on the Bridge, his body language told me that he had a nasty hangover. It was a hot, sunny day and he was also suffering from the heat. Suddenly, without warning, a huge landbird came flapping down out of the sky and settled on the winch that Evan was working on. It was an evil looking bird, similar to a vulture. It had a bald head, wicked looking beak, and a scraggy neck. The bird's presence, coupled with its unswerving stare, quite unnerved Evan and he kept shooing it away. This was to no avail as the bird simply hauled itself into the air, flew around in a circle and returned to continue its relentless staring at our unhappy Electrician. We were several hundred miles from land and found it difficult to comprehend why the bird should have been so far out to sea; nor could I explain its unusual interest in Evan. Notwithstanding, he had to endure the bird watching him until he went for his dinner at twelve 'o' clock.

In the cut and thrust of verbal jousting that went on in the Saloon I often got the better of Evan. I was in my early twenties and he was in his mid forties and I suspected that it bothered him that the last laugh was invariably mine. As far as I was concerned, anyone who made free with the barbed comments, could only expect the same, or better, in return.

Things came very unexpectedly to a head in Colombo, a port in what was then called Ceylon. I was on night duty, but as there was no cargo being worked I was sitting in my cabin. At about eleven 'o' clock there was a frenzied banging on my cabin door, nearly violent enough to break it down. Very puzzled, I got up and cautiously opened it. I was immediately on the receiving end of a vicious kick, obviously aimed at a very delicate part of my anatomy. Instinctively, I turned my body and took the kick on my thigh. The owner of the leg was a very drunken Evan Jones. In a rage, he shouted at me that I was on duty and should be on deck. That was nonsense and in any event he had no authority over me. I was furious at being kicked and he was now aiming punches at me. He was large and powerful and I was small and light; I knew that I needed space so that I could use my speed and agility in order to avoid those kicks and punches. I was completely sober so I began to reason with him; 'Look! If you really want to fight me, let's go outside on the deck where we will have plenty of space.' He readily agreed and we moved outside. Then began a real slugging match, which seemed to last a considerable time. I would sally forth, deliver a few ineffectual punches and then move out of range of his hefty punches. I couldn't hurt him, and he couldn't catch me. Very soon, most of the ship's company came to view the battle. It was obvious whose side they were on and I was in receipt of a great deal of encouragement. I knocked him to the ground several times but he just lumbered to his feet, shook his head and carried on. He knew that he couldn't catch me with his punches so he started grabbing my clothes with his left hand. Several times I tore myself free and I ended up fighting in my underpants, my flip-flops gone long ago. At one point I was banging his head on the metal accommodation bulkhead just below a porthole, when the Chief Engineer's wife popped her head out to see what all the commotion was. She promptly had hysterics.

By now I was beginning to get worried; despite my best efforts I seemed unable to stop or hurt this man. I knew that eventually I would be exhausted and then I would be beaten. My side of the fight had been reasonably clean up to that point but I decided that, as he had kicked me so viciously, I would kick him even though I was in bare-feet. The next time he went down I stuck the big toe in, so to speak. I've always felt ashamed that I actually kicked someone, but it was getting to the point that it was either him or me and this was a desperate strategy.

At this juncture, the crew quite rightly thought that Evan was going to get seriously hurt and separated us. That was the end of it, and we both retired to our cabins.

The next morning I was very popular. 'It's about time someone gave him a hammering,' I was told. I made a point of finding the Electrician. He was slumped on the deck with his head in his hands, looking battered and bruised. Wearily, he opened his eyes and looked me over. 'You bastard,' he said, 'you haven't got a mark on you.' Strictly speaking, that was untrue; the bruise on my thigh took weeks to clear up.

I decided some straight talking was needed. The gist of my blunt message was that if he ever came at me in that fashion again, he would be put over the side, one dark night, and find himself swimming back to the UK. He never bothered me again.

He did cause more trouble though, but not for me. Our stay in Colombo lasted six weeks, mainly due to a dock strike. Evan had got himself settled there and for some unknown reason was most reluctant to leave. When we were due to depart, we carried out the usual equipment checks only to discover that the rudder would not work. The Chief Engineer examined the machinery that operated it. I happened to be present when he told the Captain that he believed the mechanism had been deliberately sabotaged. The nature of the damage, he went on to say, indicated someone with electrical expertise. Repairs delayed us by a couple of days as we sourced the replacement parts needed. We eventually sailed for Australia without further incident. Of course, many of us had misgivings. We worried that if Evan were responsible for wrecking the steering gear, what else might he contemplate whilst we were at sea? Luckily, our fears were unfounded and the voyage was eventually completed without further mishap.

Being Captain of an ocean going ship is a very demanding occupation. Unlike other jobs the Captain cannot go home at five p.m. or have a weekend off. He is responsible for forty to one hundred lives, a multi-million pound ship, and the added value of its cargo.

The relentless pressure or the monotony of the long ocean voyages can take its toll. Some skippers became heavy drinkers; some had heart attacks; others simply became eccentric.

Captain Farris fitted into the latter category and was known in the Company as 'Mad Farris.' Rumours circulated that he was given command of a munitions ship during World War Two when the British were running out of ships and suitably experienced officers. Even more cruelly, some said that the people who promoted him didn't expect him to survive the War.

My first sight of him was on Bristol Railway Station. He was sitting on top of a pile of suitcases which were loaded onto an electric trolley. With his leg encased in plaster, he was waving a walking stick about as he shouted orders to the poor trolley driver escorting him to his railway carriage. 'My God,' I thought, 'who's that?' Little did I realise that we were both joining the same ship.

He was a grey haired man, in his fifties, often rude and he spoke with a drawl. My first brush with him was as we were sailing down the Bristol Channel. I went onto the Bridge at eight 'o' clock to start my watch. As usual I checked the proximity of other vessels, the position of the ship and the course on the chart. I noticed that the course line went directly over a pinnacle of rock at a depth of six fathoms. We were drawing five fathoms and there was some swell. There was deep water on either side of the rock.

I consulted the Second Mate who usually drew up the course on the chart. He told me that Captain Farris had drawn it and that I should talk to him about it. After breakfast I called the Captain onto the Bridge and drew his attention to the shallow water. He brusquely told me we had six feet of clearance, that it was perfectly safe and left the Bridge. I began to get very worried as the ship was rising and dipping in a swell, reducing our six feet clearance to near zero. This was hazardous navigation and the rock could rip the bottom out of the ship. With a slight alteration of course we would be perfectly safe. I again called the Second Mate onto the Bridge and told him that the Captain would not amend the ship's course. He gave me good advice: He told me to again call the Captain onto the Bridge, express my fears, and tell him that I was going to make an entry into the ship's logbook to that effect and that I would require him to sign it. It failed to work. I received another broadside from him and once again told to adhere to the course line on the chart.

We were due to go over the rock at about eleven a.m. At about 10:30 I decided to take the initiative myself - after all, I had nothing to lose. I knew that nudging the ship a few degrees to port we would pass well clear of the unseen rock and nobody would be any the wiser. I was just about to alter course when a very disgruntled Captain appeared on the Bridge only to disappear into the chartroom. A few moments later he reappeared and very brusquely told me to 'Go and look at the chart.' Obeying this instruction, I was very relieved to see that he had amended the course. I must have planted the seeds of doubt in his mind and, weighing the odds, he had decided to accede to my demands. Whether by design or accident he had certainly kept me sweating until very nearly the last minute.

Thus began a very difficult trip. His eyesight was bad and approaching a port at night was a very worrying time for him. He depended upon my eyes and I had to give him a running commentary of what I could see, which I found a very strange experience. Sometimes he was so worried, and under such strain, that he used to actually weep, which I found very disconcerting.

Approaching an Indian port we found ourselves in the middle of a Military Firing Practice Area, which was clearly marked on the chart. We failed in our collective attempts to persuade him to perform a 180-degree turn and get the hell out of it! He presumed that the prohibited area had been the same for years and that there was no cause for concern. Later in the morning Sparks, the Wireless Operator, came out of his shack with a message that a firing practice would begin at 10 a.m. Farris, however, decided that it was too late to take evasive action and, at precisely 10 a.m., I noticed the splash of a shell landing in the water near the ship. This continued for a nerve-wracking two hours. I can only assume the gunners were bad shots or that they were playing with us.

I think the Captain had delusions about his own expertise. One day, approaching a port, I could see on the radar a cluster of ships at anchor. Mad Farris, in his drawl told me 'I'm going to show you how to anchor Royal Navy style.' I shuddered thinking what might be the eventual outcome. The Chief Officer was sent to the fo'csal head. We steamed full speed ahead into the group of ships at anchor. The Captain ordered 'Stop engines. Drop the anchor. Full Speed Astern.' In theory this may be feasible but, in practise, life can be very different as proved to be the case. The engines continued to freewheel for some considerable time. The shocked engineers were unable to get the engines to run astern. We let out a tremendous amount of anchor cable until it was wrapped around the ship. The nearby ships, fearing a collision, began to sound their whistles, heaving up their anchors and moving out of the way. How they managed to get their engines running at such short notice we never knew. When calm had been restored and I rang 'Finished With Engines', the Captain astonished me by saying 'There, I told you I'd show you how to anchor Royal Navy style' and left the Bridge. I was left there thinking 'Do we have to hoist the Red Ensign and let everyone know we're British?'

Mad Farris was a menace at sea and an embarrassment in port. In third world countries the dockworkers earned very little money and were very poor. Farris derived childish pleasure from throwing men cigarettes and sandwiches. The sandwiches were left over from his prepared supper, which he never ate. Standing high up on the boat deck he would start by throwing one or two cigarettes. This would attract a large crowd, which was his intention. Throwing many cigarettes and sandwiches now caused scrabbling, wrestling and fighting. This spectacle caused him great amusement and he would hop about laughing excitedly.

He once asked me to go ashore with him in Port Said, Egypt to visit the Harbourmaster's Office. Off we both went dressed in smart, white tropical uniforms. We had not gone very far when a cheeky little brown boy approached us and began begging. The Captain told him to 'Bugger off' a few times but the lad was persistent. Eventually, he realised he wasn't going to get anything and became abusive. He pulled his clothing down, showed his bare behind, bent down and farted loudly. I was quite shocked, thinking that this grand figure in his impeccable Captain's uniform would be furious. To my surprise, he was highly amused and asked for a repeat performance. The boy promptly obliged and was rewarded with a handful of coins. What truly impressed me was how the boy was capable of producing the required flatulent response at will.

Our walk ashore continued to be eventful. A short time later a pimp accosted us. 'You wan' woman? I get beautiful Egyptian girl for you.'

'No, Bugger off!' was the reply.

'You wan' black girl? I get nice black girl for you.'

'No, Sod off!' The guy was persistent like the little lad. Now he wanted to procure a French girl for us. His instructions to go away became more obscene. Suddenly, with a knowing air he said 'Aaah! You wan' small boy? I get small boy for you.'

'NO! WILL YOU BUGGER OFF!' we shouted.

At this the man became quite exasperated. 'Wassa matter wid you? You don' want nice young girl. You don' want small boy. What you wan' then?'

'Well, actually,' the Captain said, 'I want the Harbourmaster.'

The man stared at him in disbelief. Eventually he said, 'Well, I try for you, but very hard.'

I think our helpless laughter made the pimp realise that he was wasting his time and he went off to pester someone else.

Captain Mad Farris was capable of the most reckless and crazy behaviour. On one memorable occasion the ship was lying at anchor off the coast of India. Because of the lack of deep water we were loading cargo from ten or twelve barges. The barges were equipped so that the workers on them could eat, sleep and work for quite a number of days. Much of their equipment was lifted onto our deck.

The Captain was in an evil mood because he had received a letter from the ship's owners. The letter reprimanded him for not leaving port promptly enough after completing cargowork.

On the last day of cargowork he was watching the proceedings very carefully. Late in the afternoon he was pacing up and down and saying to me 'Third Mate, tell me when the last sling of cargo is going in!' When I duly informed him he sent the Chief Officer to the foc'sal head and gave him orders to heave up the anchor. My position was operating the telegraph and telephones on the Bridge. I was not really sure what was going on. The hatches were still open and the cargo workers were still putting their belongings over the side into barges. Unlike me, the Captain was very certain of what he was doing. As soon as the Chief Officer informed us that the anchor was aweigh[48] I was ordered to ring 'Full Speed Ahead.' I stared at the Captain in disbelief and was promptly bawled at for the delay. 'Full Speed Ahead it is Sir!'

The effect on those on deck as they heard this command can only be imagined as an atmosphere of panic set in. As the ship began to gather speed the excited jabbering on the deck grew in volume. Men began running round the decks, throwing their equipment over the side. Every mile or so, a barge would manage to cast off and float away. I believe it was about ten miles before the last barge finally left. Looking back as far as the eye could see was a long line of barges all facing in different directions. I often wondered how they got back to harbour and how long it took them. Once again, I was left standing on the Bridge, stunned with disbelief at what I had just witnessed.

Chapter 6

Storms, Squalls, Freak Waves and Fog

When your home is rolling, lurching, dropping and lifting for days, and sometimes weeks on end, life is very uncomfortable. Luckily, I was never seasick despite sleeping, eating, and working on something akin to a fairground ride that never stopped. Every walk on the deck ran the risk of being washed overboard. Trying to sleep was difficult because my body kept rolling about in my bunk. To prevent this happening I put my pillows and rolled up clothes under one side of the mattress to create a V shaped hollow so that I could lie in the bottom of it. Wedged in this niche I was protected against the movement to some extent, though half of my body was pressed up against the wooden bulkhead, which was not very comfortable. Eating was also a challenge. Chairs and tables were secured so that they were unable to move and little rails could be lifted up around the edge of the table to prevent the crockery sliding about. By far the most effective way to prevent this was, very simply, to wet the tablecloth. Soup, tea and coffee were the most difficult to manage, because they simply flooded out of their containers as the ship rolled.

I was familiar with the notorious reputation of the Bay of Biscay and it was there, on my second voyage, that we ran into a real storm. We were punching into very heavy seas. Plunging and dipping, the whole ship would shudder and flex like someone bending a plastic ruler. Despite being made of iron and steel, the ship's elasticity in these conditions puzzled me. The bow would bury itself in the sea and then as it lifted, tons of solid seawater was thrown back across the foredeck. Numerous tiny French fishing boats bobbed about like corks on mountainous waves. If we were uncomfortable their lives must have been purgatory.

The worst was yet to come. We had a deck cargo of forty-gallon drums and in the course of a foul and tempestuous night they broke free. Brian and I had a cabin situated on the maindeck, facing forud beneath the lifeboat deck. Our cabin resonated to the booming crash of forty gallon drums as they thumped and rumbled on our metal cabin bulkhead. Some were washed overboard but others rolled forud as the ship dipped and rolled back as the ship lifted. The incessant noise in our cabin was unbearable for hour after long hour. It was like having someone strike a huge and dissonant gong adjacent to our ears. It drove me to distraction. At about three a.m., being unable to bear it any longer, I made an insane decision: I would go outside and shift the remaining drums. As rapidly as I could I pulled on my oilskins and sou'wester. Brian quite sensibly declined to join me.

To get out of the accommodation I made my way aft, along an alleyway, and opened a steel weather door. I banged at the metal clamps and eventually the door swung open.

At that precise moment we took a huge sea. The wave was so big that it passed right over the top of the lifeboat deck and tons of water slammed down in front of me. I hurriedly flung the weather door shut. My sanity returned like an express train. There was no way I would, or could, go outside onto the deck. I dejectedly slunk back to the cabin prepared to suffer for the rest of the night, and quite unprepared for what greeted my return. Silence! The huge wave had washed the remaining drums over the side. Had I been thirty seconds earlier, I would undoubtedly have shared their fate.

Next morning, breakfast was late as the galley fires needed to be re-lit. Seawater had extinguished them and, in the process, scoured the galley giving everything a strangely spotless appearance. Not only were the fires out but all the coal and ash in the stoves had vanished. A wooden barrel, full of flour had also disappeared without a trace. Not a cockroach or a weevil was to be seen, The galley doors were like those in a stable and the top halves had been left open; with no barrier to prevent it, seawater must have surged throughout the galley entirely unchecked for much of the night.

A few months later we went into dry-dock for routine repairs. The pounding we took that night in the Bay of Biscay had loosened dozens of rivets underneath the forefoot of the ship. To my astonishment they were so loose it was possible to waggle them with your finger. Such, I discovered, is the incredible power of the sea.

When it comes to bad weather, crossing the North Atlantic in winter is an awesome experience. Many of my worst voyages across this ocean took place on trampships whilst I was still an apprentice.

I well remember being in a UK port when we received orders to proceed to Norfolk, Virginia. The Able Seamen, who had been anticipating another destination, promptly left the ship – a course of action which did little for my confidence. The nature of such a crossing depends on whether the ship is fully laden, as we were on this occasion, or empty.

Well into the Atlantic the weather, as expected, turned foul. I was put on the twelve till four watch and had to take a stint on the wheel and two hours on lookout. The usual place to keep a lookout was on the foc'sal head. Here a bell is located used to send signals to the Bridge.   If we saw a light we rang the bell: one strike for a ship on the starboard bow, two for the port bow and three for a ship dead ahead. If the weather worsened, and we began shipping seas, then the lookout would be moved to the wing of the Bridge.

Out on the wild ocean in the middle of a dark night one's imagination can begin to play tricks. Some of the sailors became scared because they said that the bell was ringing of its own accord. They requested to be allowed to do their lookout duty on the wing of the Bridge for the whole of their watch. I was extremely sceptical regarding ghosts or bells that ring in the middle of the night so I continued to do my duty on the foc'sal head. However, my self confidence on this score was about to be seriously dented.

This voyage was my first experience of Atlantic squalls. Up on the foc'sal the visibility would be quite good as the ship rolled gently along. With very little warning a kind of mini storm would suddenly arrive. The howl of the wind would be accompanied by torrential rain; the ship would start rolling violently whilst lightning sizzled amongst the masts and rigging, followed by deafening thunder. Trying to keep a lookout was impossible because of the blinding rain and sleet. Generally these squalls, though vicious, would only last minutes so I would find what shelter I could. At times like this I would dream of my family, my home and my friends. My body would be in one place but my mind was transported thousands of miles away.

It was during one of these violent squalls and dreamlike state that the bell rang twice. I was so absorbed in my mental wanderings that a single thought floated through my mind 'Ship on the port bow.' Suddenly, shockingly, I was back on board ship. In horror my brain shouted at me 'That bell rang! I'm on the foc'sal head and I didn't ring it!' My hair stood on end; I was frozen to the spot. Slowly I began to recover my composure and the conversation in my brain continued. 'Is someone playing a joke on me?' I wondered. No, nobody would have ventured on the foredeck at this ungodly hour. 'Should I go back to the Bridge and tell them that I haven't seen a light and that I didn't ring the bell?' I wondered. 'No,' I concluded, 'they'll think I've gone mad, and anyway I'll have to walk right past that damned bell.'

Logic and reason began to re-establish themselves. A bell does not just ring by itself; something must have made it ring. The squall was still in full force with a beam wind of gale strength. If the wind and the rolling of the ship combined, then that would be sufficient for the clapper to strike the bell. Yes! That was it! Panic over. I stared in the direction of the bell and sure enough, in the brief eerie illumination of the lightning flashes, I could see the bell rope waving wildly.

At the end of my lookout duty, I felt I ought to visit the Second Mate on the Bridge to explain that I had not seen a light. He seemed puzzled. 'Well, I didn't think you had,' he said, 'I didn't hear you ring the bell.' I went to my bunk feeling rather uneasy that night. Were the sailors right? Was the bell ringing itself? And, if so, why was the Second Mate on the Bridge unable to hear it?

In the following days the weather deteriorated even further and the sea became rougher. Movement along the deck became quite dangerous. In hindsight I cannot understand why lifelines were never rigged. It just seemed that all safety measures were treated with scorn.

On my afternoon watch, apart from a spell on the wheel, I was obliged to go and join the other dayworkers. As no work was possible on the deck we were all under the foc'sal head cleaning paintbrushes and completing other jobs that were usually neglected. Movement along the deck was hazardous. It was a case of noting which was the weatherside of the ship, studying the frequency of waves and running with all the speed you could muster along the heaving deck as soon as the opportunity arose. When your life depended on it, you soon became good at it.

Engineers rarely ventured on deck so they were not good at dodging the waves. One day we saw that, for some unusual reason, the fourth engineer was heading in our direction. This drew quite a lot of interest and wicked speculation on what the outcome might be. We were not to be disappointed. Initially, he made the wise choice of selecting the sheltered side of the ship. I noted that he was smoking a cigarette. He passed number two hatch safely but disaster struck passing number one. He spotted a huge wave coming over the weather side and looked round wild-eyed. He searched desperately about and, to his relief, saw an eyebolt near his feet. Immediately he crouched down, grabbing it with both hands. As he did so the ice-cold sea cascaded heavily over the top of him. Happily, when the sea cleared he was still there. He was a comical sight with the cigarette still in his mouth but now sodden and drooping. His hair looked as though it had been combed and plastered to his face. Gathering himself, he quickly continued his journey and arrived in the foc'sal head saturated, and shivering with the cold. He could have gained little comfort from our cruel laughter.

As if in retribution I nearly came to grief myself later that day. At four p.m. I finished work and set off back to my cabin. No sooner was I out of the foc'sal head than we shipped a huge wave, referred to by sailors as a 'green un.' Panic-stricken I looked in all directions for an escape. My only option it seemed was to run up the ladder onto the foc'sal head despite the fact that, as every sailor knows, in heavy weather this is usually the most dangerous location on the ship. The Bosun, realising that I must be in trouble, poked his head out of the foc'sal and shouted 'John! John! Where are you?' By this time I was on the foc'sal head above him clinging to a rail for grim death. 'I'm up here' I shouted pathetically. The look of kind concern turned to fury when he caught sight of me. 'What the bloody hell are you doing up there?' In the bluntest of terms he suggested I took myself elsewhere. Fortunately, my second attempt to gain the safety of my cabin was more successful.

The problems of crossing the North Atlantic in winter on an empty ship are quite different from those experienced when fully laden. Obviously the Captain takes on plenty of seawater ballast in an attempt to get the ship lower in the water. However, the ship's side acts like a huge sail and the propeller and rudder continuously jump out of the water in rough weather. This makes it difficult to steer the ship and causes the engine to race wildly. Paradoxically, because of their height above the water the decks are normally dry and safe.

We were crossing the North Atlantic on an old tub of a trampship that could only manage a maximum of ten knots in the best of conditions. For a week or more the wind strength was Force Nine and above. Towering, mountainous seas had built up. It is very difficult to calculate the size of waves but these were enormous by any standard. We are talking here of a ten thousand ton ship of about 600 feet in length. When she dropped into a trough between two waves, there appeared to be a huge hill of water on either side. I maintain that had I been able to climb to the very truck[50] of the topmast I would not have been able to see over the crest of these waves. This would suggest waves in the region of ninety feet, in other words as high, or higher, than the average church tower. Watching other large vessels, disappearing completely out of sight, masts, funnel and all when sinking into a trough, provides further evidence of the probable size of these waves. I am well aware that marine scientists would say that this is far fetched, but recent satellite observations are beginning to prove the existence of huge waves previously thought impossible.

When in the bottom of one of these troughs I felt that we would never survive and that we would be overwhelmed by vast amounts of water. Happily, the ship would float steadily up the side of a hill of water until we were perched on the crest. It was so mind boggling and so spectacular that I never felt afraid.

However, it was not the size of the waves that caused the problems, but the wind. As a result we were unable to steer and frequently blown off course as the ship refused to respond to the helm. We were obliged to display special signals: two large, black balls by day and two all round red lights at night. This was a warning to other vessels that we were 'Not Under Command.'; in other words they had to keep out of our way because we could not keep out of theirs. Frequently, arriving to relieve the man on the wheel, I would be told, 'I've had the rudder hard over for two hours and she won't answer.' Our record for having the rudder hard over, and not being able to get the ship on course, was forty-eight hours.

Some days we made no progress through the water at all and so the crossing became a very long one. Sparks, listening on his radio, was able to tell us that during this unusually violent weather, the Queen Elizabeth passed us three times. She was the fastest ship in the world at that time.

On a similar voyage across the North Atlantic we had a very alarming experience. On this occasion it was not blowing hard but we had a rough, following sea. Because we were a light ship the decks were completely dry and the sun was shining. I was on day work and at ten-thirty in the morning we had all gone for 'Smoko' which in my case was a foul cup of coffee. The important point to note here, is by sheer good fortune, no one was on the deck.

Safe and relaxed in the officers' smoking room, I was standing with a cup of coffee in my hand. Looking aft along an alleyway I was astonished to see a wall of water coming towards me; it all happened so quickly that I did not even have time to be frightened. A simple thought flashed through my mind that my end had come. Inexplicably, the water did not even knock me off my feet but flowed out of the room as quickly and unexpectedly as it had come. I was left standing, totally drenched, and clutching my cup, now filled with seawater. It transpired that a freak wave had come unnoticed over the poop and flooded the sailors' accommodation. Rushing along the main deck it surged through the cabins under the Bridge where I had been drinking my coffee, continuing along the foredeck where it caught Chippy[50] in his workshop underneath the foc'sal head. Fortunately, he saw the wave coming and, having no other option, simply grabbed the handles of his vice as he was drenched from head to toe. He showed me that his workshop must have been completely full of seawater pointing to the sawdust and shavings which still adhered to the top of the bulkhead and deckhead.

There was no damage: the worst problem was in the crew accommodation where drawers had been filled with water and some, completely dislodged, were floating amidst a bedraggled mass of sodden clothing. Fortunately, no-one was lost overboard because not a soul was on deck. It is worth mentioning that had the hatches been open we should have foundered instantly, joining the list of sizeable ships that have just vanished without trace. An hour later the decks were bone dry again and remained so for the rest of that day; we were not even troubled by spray. Recovering from the shock of my experience I considered myself fortunate to have survived to tell the tale.

Chippy the carpenter, saved from injury or worse by his quick thinking, was a dour Scot. A fine craftsman and one of dying breed, he very rarely used a tape measure. He seemed able to mentally calculate how long a piece of wood needed to be and then simply cut it. Small and stocky, his face badly scarred with black lines, he walked with a limp. I never ever saw him without his flat cap, and rumour had it that he even slept in it. He was a stubborn and independent man and reckless regarding his own safety. For example, we noticed that he was not particularly prudent when moving along the deck in heavy weather; nothing would stop him from going where he wanted to go. This attitude had cost him dearly. According to some of the sailors who had known him for many years, he had, on one occasion, been washed overboard by number one hatch but luckily deposited back on board at number five. This experience left him badly injured, hence the limp. However, his body might have been battered, but not his spirit - he was still just as reckless as before his accident.

I was very curious about the scars on his face and, when I felt I knew him well enough, I asked him what had caused them. As mentioned previously, the scars were like lines, deeply scored and etched with black, running from the bottom of his face towards the top. His nose was particularly affected.

He explained that, at the end of a particularly arduous voyage, the sailors, including him, had gone ashore and become hopelessly drunk. Sailors will always look after their own, even someone not considered a friend. Returning to the ship could often become a mopping up operation; if one came across a shipmate staggering about through drink or injury, he was assured of immediate support.

Two sailors rolling back to the ship, much the worse for drink, came across Chippy lying face down on the pavement unable to regain his feet. They decided he was in need of their help and, seizing a leg each, began dragging him, still face down, back to the ship. By the time he was conscious enough to stop them, the damage had been done. His face was wrecked. The black lines under his skin were caused by the abrasion of the dirt ground in from the pavement, creating a kind of unwanted hideous tattoo. Chippy's reflection was as droll as it was philosophical, 'From now on, if I'm ever going to pass out, I'll make sure I'll fall on my back!'

In the days of sailing ships one could imagine that it was not uncommon for vessels to run out of food and water. Voyages would take substantially longer than expected if the winds were unfavourable or indeed, if there were no winds at all. One would not expect this to happen on steamships and motor vessels during the twentieth century. However, on a voyage from Long Beach, California to Hamburg, we had experienced bad weather the whole way, the effect of which was to substantially reduce our speed. The Chief Steward, perhaps attempting to avoid the high cost of food in Long Beach, had not even considered the possibility of unforeseen circumstances extending the voyage.

The first inkling we had that something was amiss with our food supplies was when we began being served rather a lot of veal. It was appearing on the menu twice a day, and after four or five days, featured on the breakfast menu too. The situation worsened as daily the amount and variety of food diminished. Eventually, we ran out of food completely. There were no cereals, bread, milk, coffee or even tea. Water was available but we had now ceased to sit down for any kind of meal.

The sailors were convinced that the Officers were still being served food and the atmosphere grew quite volatile. To defuse the situation, the Chief Steward invited the sailors to inspect his storerooms. I went along to see for myself only to discover that his larder was entirely comprised of numerous jars of pickled onions. Not a satisfactory state of affairs for a starving crew.

Eventually we made landfall within sight of the coastline of England. One might have thought that the Old Man would put into port, or anchor nearby and have some food sent on board, but he did not do so. To make matters worse we broke down and anchored off Beachy Head to carry out engine repairs. Small coasters were passing quite close by and the crew were shouting, half jokingly, half seriously, 'Any chance of a loaf of bread mate?' No one responded or even heard us, I suspect.

After about six hours we weighed anchor and continued to Hamburg. The Captain radioed ahead and when we docked at one a.m., a hot meal was awaiting us on the quayside. It was three days since we had eaten anything at all. Apart from being ravenously hungry, which I always was anyway, at the age of eighteen, I cannot say that I suffered any ill effects of any sort.

From Hamburg we proceeded to the U.K and Brian and I were allowed leave for a few days. Before we left the Captain asked us not to tell our parents that we had run out of food. I think that was the only time he showed the slightest bit of concern for our welfare. Of course, we did tell our parents, and were quite proud of having survived our minor ordeal of starvation. We made jokes about renaming the ship the 'S.S. Hardship'.

Fog at sea is very frightening. Whilst in Buenos Aires I went to look at a ship that had limped into port following a collision with another vessel in thick fog. The damage was extensive. There was a hole in the bow that was so big it would have been possible to drive two double decker buses side by side into the aperture. Despite this, the ship was floating on an even keel, without any sign of a list. The ship had survived in this state only because a special collision bulkhead had not been breached.

Prior to the introduction of radar, movement in fog, particularly in congested waters, gave rise to great concern. Vessels of all nationalities were, and still are, required to give a fog signal as prescribed in 'The International Regulations for Preventing Collision At Sea.' By listening out for signals sounded on whistles and bells, it is possible to know whether nearby ships are moving, stopped or at anchor.

Once ships were equipped with radar, fog lost some of its trepidation. It was now possible to locate other ships on the radar screen and know exactly how far away they were. Unfortunately, the blip on the screen did not indicate the direction in which the ship was travelling, or whether it had changed its course or speed. A new phenomenon occurred, known as the 'radar assisted collision'. Navigating officers like me were hurriedly sent on courses so that we could work out exactly what nearby ships were doing.

The ship's fog signal nearly drove us mad and some found it impossible to sleep. If one stands next to a lighthouse during fog, the deafening languid honk of the foghorn gives a precise idea of what it is like being on-board ship during restricted visibility.

My first experience of fog was in the Strait of Dover. We did not have radar and were unsure of our position. All around us ships were sounding their fog signals and the Captain decided to stop and drop anchor. Our fog signal now changed to the rapid ringing of a bell so nearby ships would know we were at anchor.

We remained in this state, with other ships feeling their way past us, until the fog cleared. The Second Mate took some bearings of shore objects and put a position on the chart which, to our alarm, showed that we were anchored right over a submarine cable, probably telephone wires. The Captain was not in the slightest bit concerned as he was of the view that there was very little chance of us picking it up. The Chief Officer was ordered to heave up the anchor only to discover that, contrary to the Captain's opinion, the cable was lying across its flukes[51]. Several attempts were made to dislodge the cable by dropping the anchor and heaving it up again; the cable remained stubbornly caught. Eventually a man was put over the side in a bosun's chair[52]. A line was then looped round the cable and secured; the anchor was then lowered and the cable became disentangled and dropped back into the seabed. I have often wondered whether important messages between the British and French Governments were mysteriously interrupted that day. I think it highly unlikely that we reported our faux pas.

A few years later I had a very unpleasant experience in the Bristol Channel. I was coasting with a very well known company, moving from ship to ship, relieving officers whilst they went home on leave. This was quite easy but not very pleasant, as I did not know the ships, the Captains or the other relieving officers very well.

At one point I was relieving on a huge twin screw freezer ship. One morning we were proceeding down the Bristol Channel when thick fog came down. Immediately, following standard practice in these situations, I switched on both the radar and the fog signal. As the ship was fitted with automatic steering, I was entirely alone on the Bridge. My first fog signal brought an immediate response from the Captain as I expected it would. I received quite a shock when, instead of remaining on the Bridge to assume command, as was customary, he simply ordered me to stop sounding the fog signal. 'Use of the radar is enough,' he said, and disappeared. I was quite concerned because, here we were, thundering down the Bristol Channel at seventeen knots in the fastest ship I had ever served on - but in zero visibility.

Later in the morning I put the engines on standby as the radar indicated a good deal of shipping in our vicinity. This was a warning to the engineers that I might stop, or slow down. You could hear the telegraph ring almost all over the ship and I knew that, once again, the Captain would appear on the Bridge. Without saying a word to me he studied the radar, put the engines back on 'Full Ahead' and told me not to put the engines on standby again without his permission. Once again he left the Bridge. Needless to say, I was extremely relieved when the Second Mate took over at noon.

A few months later, in the early hours of the morning, one of our ships was lost in the Mediterranean, having hit a reef and sinking almost immediately. About ninety sailors lost their lives; only seven or eight of the crew survived. One of them was the Captain, the same man whose behaviour in the Bristol Channel I had considered criminally negligent.

CHAPTER 7

Mayday Mayhem

As a teenager, prior to the advent of television, I was an avid reader of sea adventure stories. I was fascinated by seamen and explorers, including such well known names as Captain Bligh of the Bounty, Captain Cook and Sir Ernest Shackleton. Subconsciously, in joining the Merchant Navy, I no doubt nurtured the secret hope that I too might be involved in heroic rescues or other dramas at sea. I had been well trained in lifeboat skills, fire fighting, and man overboard procedures and in some way this perpetuated my belief that my chosen career would one day bring me adventure and excitement. The reality was, shall we say, somewhat different.

I had just joined a tanker and was signed on as Third Mate. We quickly left port and soon we were proceeding along the English Channel in the most hostile conditions. Visibility was good but the head seas were snappy and snarling with a wind so strong that the ship was shuddering and vibrating as the powerful engines strained to force us through the water.

At about eight-thirty p.m. Sparks came out of his shack with news of a 'Mayday' call. A ship had got into difficulties and was calling for assistance; more than that we didn't know. I laid its position off on the chart and noted that it was only about thirty miles away, about two hours steaming.

I called up the Captain who in turn sent for the Chief Officer and the Second Mate. The Engineers were informed so that they would be ready to alter speed, stop, and if necessary, go astern. It was decided that the Chief Officer would take charge of the boatdeck, and the Second Mate and some sailors would lower a lifeboat if required. I was to stay on the Bridge with the Captain, extremely relieved that I would not be needed to take charge of a lifeboat. Lowering a lifeboat from a ship tied up to the quayside in calm conditions is hazardous enough, let alone in a howling gale. What the Second Mate was feeling like I could only imagine.

Having altered course we began to scrutinise the radar screen. The Captain, I noticed, was continually leaving the Bridge for a few minutes at a time. This puzzled me until I smelt alcohol on his breath, a turn of events which alarmed me considerably. I was a junior officer with almost no experience of ship handling in conditions such as these. Once near the stricken vessel, we would need to stop, provide shelter for our lifeboat and later pick it up again. Each of these actions carried substantial risk, as once we were stationary the wind would rapidly blow us toward the crippled ship. The Captain was obviously having the same thoughts and his solution was to drink himself insensible. What was I to do? Should I call up the Chief Officer and tell him that the Captain was drunk? No, I decided, he had problems of his own. As we neared the vessel in distress, I could see on the radar that many other ships were approaching it too. The Captain was further inebriated, slurring his words and, to my mind, incapable of making rational decisions.

By the time we reached the vessel in trouble its lights were indistinguishable from those of the small township of craft surrounding it. Almost at the moment of our arrival on scene Sparks received a message saying that the Mayday call was cancelled. I have never been so relieved in my whole life. As quickly as our adventure began it was over, and we could return to the less fraught business of our voyage. The Captain, who I subsequently discovered generally accounted for a bottle of gin each day, promptly went to bed and it was not long before the others followed him. I was left to continue my watch and to ruminate on the evening's events.

One often reads complaints from people who have been shipwrecked, that several large vessels have passed really close by, yet they have not been seen. I cannot understand how they and their frantic signals have been missed as, in the vastness of the ocean, I was able to locate the tiniest speck when it was ten or fifteen miles away.

One beautiful sunny morning in the middle of the South Atlantic I noticed just such a speck on the far horizon. I studied it closely for some considerable time and decided that it was a tiny cabin cruiser, though what it could be doing there was beyond my comprehension. I followed the usual procedure of calling the Captain and he put the engines on standby. Gradually we slowed to a halt, by which time the little boat was just a few feet away under the wing of the Bridge. It was motionless in the water and from our lofty vantage point bore no sign of life. As it lay there, wallowing in the swell, I had ghastly visions of dehydrated corpses, inert and emaciated in the cabin. What should we do now? The Captain, who had seen it all before, had no hesitation whatsoever. He gave a long piercing blast on the ship's whistle. To my astonishment, two startled oriental gentlemen popped out of the cabin, rubbing their bleary eyes in the bright, tropical sunshine. They had obviously fallen asleep. Then followed some unintelligible communication between us, and through this curious semaphore the Captain evidently gathered they were in no distress and did not require our assistance. The telegraph clanged as he ordered 'Full Ahead Engines.'

'I don't understand, Sir. Why have we left them?' I asked, still puzzled.

'Well,' he said, 'they are fishermen. There will be a mother ship somewhere. Each morning dozens of little boats will be launched to fish all day and return at sunset with their catch. Those two rascals are skiving instead of working.'

Local knowledge of this sort, acquired over many years at sea, was absolutely invaluable in making sense of otherwise inexplicable events. This was no more true than on one memorable occasion when we were sailing in the Persian Gulf. It was unbearably hot, flat calm, and without a breath of wind. I had spotted an Arab dhow, which was obviously becalmed. From its deck came a cacophony of clashing sound, and I could discern the crew members beating pans and other metal objects for all they were worth. Baffled, I called the Captain who immediately identified the cause. 'They've run out of drinking water. That racket is to attract our attention.'

We stopped the ship, put a hose over the side and filled all their containers. Not a very dramatic event, but nevertheless a very important one to the Arab crew who might have died of thirst had it not been for the local knowledge which had brought us to their aid.

My own efforts to mount a dramatic maritime rescue, on the other hand, caused much hilarity amongst the ship's company. On a voyage from

Cape Town to Brazil I was particularly bored because we had not seen any shipping for a week. On the morning in question the weather was perfect, with cloudless skies, pleasantly warm with crystal clear visibility. I was on watch and keeping a sharp lookout when I spotted a dot on the horizon. I studied the object through my binoculars with growing interest and decided that it was something unusual. Eventually, after much scrutiny I concluded that it was, unbelievably, three black men in a canoe. What in God's name could three black men be doing out here about five hundred miles from land? They could only be survivors from some kind of shipwreck.

I telephoned the Captain and said 'You're not going to believe this Sir, but I've spotted three black men in a canoe.' He arrived promptly on the Bridge and immediately seizing my binoculars and studying the speck, declared 'My God, you're right Third Mate.' Immediately the whole ship was put on standby and, presuming that the men might be weak and exhausted, we had a lifeboat and pilot ladder made ready. The entire crew turned out on deck to watch this dramatic spectacle as I, struggling to contain my excitement, anticipated at long last being a key player in a real maritime rescue.

As we got nearer I continued to examine the three men in the canoe. They were clearly exhausted and must have been close to the limits of survival as they were no longer paddling; perhaps even more worrying was the fact that they made no movement at all. I was beginning to entertain the notion that we were too late, that somehow they were dead already when, staring at them through my binoculars, I could see that each of them had an unusually large and distinctive nose. Suddenly overwhelmed with sickening embarrassment I realised that the full blown rescue mission I had instigated to save the lives of three desperate sailors had been prompted by nothing more than three large black birds, perched on a convenient piece of timber.

My discomfort was complete as, within minutes, we sailed alongside the object of our rescue mission. Forty crewmembers stared in amused disbelief as the three feathered castaways stared blankly back from the safety of their log, probably part of a trampship's deck cargo washed overboard in a passing storm. They did not even have the decency to fly away.

For days the crew spoke of little else; my humanitarian mission was the cause of considerable mirth and I was teased mercilessly. There was nowhere to hide.

However, my story is not entirely comprised of heroic failure. I did once manage to give another vessel some much-needed assistance. At the time we were sailing along the East Coast of South Africa near Durban. It was a dark, foggy night but with the help of our radar I could clearly see the jagged indentations of the coastline.

Sparks came onto the Bridge and told me that he was communicating in Morse code with a nearby ship. Their radar had broken down, he said, and they were stationary in very shallow water, unaware of their precise position and courting potential disaster if they strayed towards the rocky coastline. Luckily, technology had moved on and we were equipped with V.H.F radio and I was able to make contact with them. From the tone of his voice I could tell that the chap on the other end was extremely worried. Fortunately for him, there was only one blip on my radar screen so his ship was easy to identify. Knowing my own position exactly I was able to take a bearing and distance of the blip and work out a precise location. Within a very short time I gave them their latitude and longitude over the V.H.F. The worry betrayed in the voice on the radio earlier was replaced by relief and gratitude. I had obviously lifted a great weight from his shoulders. He was actually about five miles from the land, but in the thick fog, he had no means of knowing this.

We wished each other 'Bon Voyage, Good Luck and Good Night' and sailed on, strangers passing in the night. This was more like it, the satisfied glow derived from helping fellow sailors in a spot of bother. I went to my bunk that night with a feeling of a job well done.

Ships, with the exception of large passenger ships and warships, do not carry doctors, policemen, or firemen. Whatever problems occur have to be resolved by the crew with the limited resources at their disposal. With this in mind, and in acknowledgement of the fact that serious fires can occur on ships, I was sent on a fire-fighting course to Speke Aerodrome, Liverpool. It was a really good, hands on course where, initially, we learnt to identify the three elements necessary for a fire to burn - heat, oxygen and combustible material. Remove one of these three and the fire will be extinguished. This was followed by practical experience of putting out 'real' fires using water or foam.

The culmination of the course was quite a terrifying experience. A ship's hold had been simulated consisting of four huge metal compartments. Two were positioned on top of the other two and an oil fire was started in one of the lower compartments which filled them all with smoke. Wearing breathing apparatus and full protective clothing, we were required, in turn, to extinguish the oil fire. To do this, we had to climb on top of the compartments and enter one of them through a trapdoor. Dragging a hose, we then had to identify a door into the other top compartment. We were now in total darkness which is something we rarely experience. Once in the second compartment we had to find a hole in the floor with a ladder leading down to a lower compartment. Still dragging the hose and feeling our way, we had to locate a doorway which would give us access to the last compartment containing the oil fire. All this was done without a light of any kind. Finally, we had to extinguish the fire with a fine, 'fog' spray of water.

The breathing apparatus, the smoke, the utter darkness and the searing heat from the fire combined to make it a nerve-wracking and unforgettable experience. Some men just refused to even enter the first compartment; others got half way round, panicked and banged the nozzle of the hose on the side of the compartment. This was the pre-arranged signal to the instructors, an indication that they had had enough. The compartments were fitted with huge doors that could be opened in an instant, enabling the smoke to clear in seconds revealing a would-be fire fighter, scared out of his wits. Enclosed spaces or total darkness have never concerned me: my problem was the damned hose. Although someone was feeding it in at the top, I was not strong enough to pull it around all the corners. I kept having to crawl back on my hands and knees, feeling my way along the hose to pull myself more slack. By the time I reached the fire I was nearly fainting from the heat.

Getting back to my ship, the Chief Officer was very keen to utilise my newly acquired skills by way of a 'Fire Drill. Now hailed as the 'expert', I was selected to try out the 'smoke helmet.' The smoke helmet was similar to the breathing apparatus except that the air was supplied through an air line fed by bellows. Unfortunately, no one realised that the smoke helmet was brand new and, before leaving the factory, had been liberally treated with French chalk — a very fine white powder.

The helmet was placed over my head and the fastenings made secure. Responding to my confident thumbs up sign the bellows operators began pumping with a will and immediately I was enveloped in choking, swirling powder. Coughing and spluttering and peering through a white haze, I was desperate to remove the helmet. By the time I was rescued my hair and face were completely white. Far from offering sympathy at my plight the response of my shipmates was to double up with helpless laughter.

The Chief Officer now turned his attention to an emergency fire pump. There was one in the engine room which was, of course, started by the engineers themselves; we also had another pump situated in a compartment housing the steering machinery. The thinking was that if there was a fire in the engine room, causing the pump located there to be put out of action, a second pump positioned elsewhere on the ship would provide vital back up. This pump needed to be started manually because a fire could disable all the ship's generators.

In order to provide us with the skills we might need in an emergency the Chief Officer quite rightly decided that our training should include starting the fire pump. This was a diesel engine, complete with compression levers and an old-fashioned starting handle. Looking around for likely volunteers the Chief's eye fell upon me and, before I knew it I was swinging the starting handle. With a few energetic yanks I had the engine turning over quite quickly, and when the Chief threw the compression levers over, the engine fired. The starting handle promptly flew off and hit me on the forehead.

I confess that gave me a fair old whack and I immediately covered the spot with my hand. 'It often does that,' the Chief Officer said weakly.

'Well I wish you'd bloody well warned me,' I retorted. When I removed my hand from my forehead, which was now pouring blood, the Chief looked horror struck, his face as white as a sheet. 'My God,' I thought, as the blood ran freely from the gash and I instinctively clapped my hand to my head once more. The Chief looked as though he was about to faint.

In a state of great consternation he escorted me to his cabin where I persuaded him to give me a large tot of rum. A taxi was hastily summoned to ferry me to the nearest casualty unit where nine stitches were inserted.

Whilst I was being treated, the Doctor decided to give me a tetanus injection which seemed a sensible precaution. Over the next few days things were getting back to normal when, waking up one morning, I discovered a lump on my forearm the size and shape of half an egg. I assumed that I had been bitten by some kind of insect, but after breakfast I was astonished to find an identical lump on my other forearm. As the morning wore on I rapidly developed lumps and blotches all over my body.

Luckily, although we were due to sail the next day, we were still in the U.K. and I made several visits to the Captain to tell him that I was ill, but he would have none of it. He thought I was malingering and simply attempting to avoid serving on the ship. In desperation I stripped off my shirt in his cabin and once he caught sight of my chest and waist he acted quickly. A taxi was called and I was taken to be examined by a Harley Street specialist.

The specialist's diagnosis was brief but dramatic, 'Giant urticaria, hospital straight away.' I was stunned, largely because I had never heard of urticaria, large or small, and assumed, judging by my alarming symptoms, it must be something serious. What he failed to explain was that my condition was caused by an adverse reaction to the tetanus injection.

He was adamant that I should go to hospital straight away but reluctantly allowed me to return briefly to the ship to collect my clothes and precious sextant. I didn't realise how ill I was. By the time I had packed my suitcases I was completely confused and had no idea what I was doing. A label with my name on it was pinned to my sleeve, along with an envelope from the specialist, and I was taken to the Merchant Navy Officers' Hospital in Greenwich by taxi. I have no recollection of the following three days but after ten days I was declared completely cured and free to go home. The Captain had nearly bullied me into sailing on the ship and I have often wondered what would have become of me had I gone.

However there did come a day when my fire-fighting skills were called upon. We were discharging thousands of tons of baled cotton in Liverpool. The Mersey ports had suffered some devastating cotton fires and so we were even more alert than usual. It was Saturday and we were having our dinner as the dockers were closing the hatches for the weekend. Suddenly a docker poked his head through the Saloon doors and shouted 'Smell of smoke in number three hatch, Chief!'

The Saloon emptied as if someone had shouted 'Abandon ship!' We all piled down the hatch sniffing and searching. Almost immediately I found a red-hot glowing patch, about the size of a tea plate on top of a bale of cotton. The Chief Officer was nearby so I shouted 'Over here Sir.' He came rushing over and we were both aware that the bale might explode into flames at any moment and the resulting fire could prove extremely serious. The burning cotton was almost certainly the result of someone thoughtlessly stubbing out a cigarette.

The Chief Officer, looking extremely concerned yelled 'John, go and get a fire extinguisher.' In our rush to locate the fire no one had thought of bringing one down with us. This was certainly not the occasion to debate whether we should use dry powder, foam, water or CO_2 as I realised instantly that time was of the essence. 'No need Sir,' I said, because nature had provided me with my own fire extinguisher. I unzipped my trousers and, without further ado, urinated onto the smouldering cotton. With a loud hissing noise and a thoroughly unpleasant odour the fire was put out. The Chief Officer looked somewhat taken aback but did not remonstrate with me. 'My God, did they teach you that on your fire fighting course?' he asked me.

'No Sir,' I returned, surprised by my own enterprise, ' just came to me all of sudden.'

My unorthodox method of fighting fires was the cause of great debate, and much ribald comment; like my daring rescue of the three black birds, it provided the crew with more than enough material to rib me for days on end.

Thankfully I was never involved in a 'man overboard' emergency though it had been part of my training. The problem with a man falling overboard at sea is finding him again. In the dark it can be a hopeless task, and even in daylight a man can be completely obscured for much of the time by waves or swell. Once the alarm has been sounded, a ship will have covered some considerable distance. Putting the rudder hard over and performing a one hundred and eighty degree turn, the ship will not be retracing its path. Large ships have a huge turning circle.

On each wing of the Bridge there is a lifebelt housed in a special case, with a light attached. With the shout of 'Man Overboard' the Officer on the Bridge pulls out a wooden pin and the lifebelt rolls out of its case into the water taking the light with it. On hitting the water the light floats the right way up and is illuminated. The job of locating the man in the water is then made much easier, especially if he can swim to the lifebelt.

I was an unwilling participant in a man overboard farce in Galle, Sri Lanka. We were at anchor waiting to start cargowork. Sri Lanka is a beautiful tropical island surrounded by clear blue water teeming with all manner of sea life including large sharks and even the odd sea snake. Despite this, swimming from the beaches is considered quite safe.

It was customary for me to have a couple of hours sleep during the afternoon prior to going on anchor watch until midnight. I knew there was a drinking party going on somewhere because I could hear the occasional crescendo of raucous voices and laughter. Drunken discussions had led, for reasons best known only to themselves, to the topic of man overboard drill. In their befuddled state, they decided it would be a good idea to stage the real thing. But who should be their hapless victim? It had to be someone who was a good swimmer ....

I was snoozing happily in my bunk clad only in a pair of brief shorts. Suddenly, I found myself being carted shoulder high, out onto the deck, across to the rail, then dumped unceremoniously over the side into the sea. I had no clue what was going on but came quickly to my senses as I hit the water. Luckily, there was no tide or current running and I began to swim around in circles whilst, in my mind, a picture of the shark I had seen the previous day was beginning to form. I had read too many stories about shark attacks to feel comfortable. It was also very strange to be looking up at my own huge ship, feeling very small and vulnerable in the water.

Having thrown me into the sea, a drunken debate ensued regarding what should be done next. Somebody produced a lifebelt and threw it in my general direction but the line was so short that it did not even reach the water and it just swung crazily about on the ship's side. I started shouting for a pilot ladder so that I could climb out, but they would not agree to it because they considered it was cheating. Someone managed to lengthen the line on the lifebelt sufficiently so that it was able reach me in the water. Grabbing the line I managed to wriggle my way into the lifebelt so that it was secure beneath my armpits. The drunken party on deck then proceeded to drag me unceremoniously out of the water, up the ship's side and onto the deck - a very uncomfortable journey, to say the least. The practice drill over, laughing and arguing, they returned to their drinking and I to my bunk. In my early days at sea I had dreamed of playing a part in a man overboard drama. Earlier that afternoon, when I had first stretched out on my bunk, I had no idea that my dream was about to become a sudden reality nor that it would be me in the starring role.

Chapter 8

A Girl in Every Port?

After a long voyage at sea, the prospect of arriving in port, getting dressed up and going ashore was very appealing. Life at sea was often boring and unnatural, starved as we were of female company and unable to visit a pub, cinema, theatre or restaurant. It was always a pleasure to step off the ship to explore ports in countries that I had never visited before, especially if they had cultures very different from our own.

As one can imagine, forty healthy men very much wanted to have a drink and meet members of the opposite sex. I soon found out that I could only meet girls in bars or in the Mission to Seamen or Catholic Flying Angel Club. The former attempted to relieve you of your money as quickly as possible, the latter were really nice, respectable girls who would not normally meet you outside of a seaman's club.

In the fifties we grew up much less streetwise than the children of today. Just as at sixteen I had to learn very quickly to be streetwise, I also had to learn to be portwise. My learning curve in this respect was largely constructed of humorous or disastrous mistakes. There was no doubt that some ports, even in the so-called civilised countries, could be very dangerous.

I remember, with some amusement in Mombasa, Kenya, two sailors were returning to the ship in the early hours of the morning much the worse for drink. Set upon by a gang of locals, stripped of almost everything they had, they had little alternative but to continue their journey in bare feet and underpants. Of course, everyone thought it was a huge joke and told them that they were lucky to have been left in their underwear.

After one month at sea I had learned some fearful language. On home leave, when the whole family was sitting at the dinner table, I called one of my brothers, 'A dirty little whore.' There was a shocked silence from my parents. Later my father very gravely asked me if I knew what a whore was. I had to admit, rather shamefacedly, that I didn't. 'Well, it means a loose woman and it's not a nice word. Don't use it again.' I went away very puzzled thinking 'What on earth is a loose woman?'

When Brian and I were both seventeen we went ashore in a port called Savona in Italy. At that age we weren't really drinkers so we wandered about trying to find something to do. In one street, we saw a huge queue, apparently waiting to get into a cinema and thought it would be a good idea to see the film, even if it was in a foreign language. We failed to notice that the queue was solely older men but after a considerable time we eventually reached the ticket kiosk. When we asked for our tickets the lady in the kiosk shouted at us loudly, jabbering rapidly. It was obvious we were not welcome, and very puzzling and embarrassing until we realised that we had been trying to get into a state run bordello where they operated a strict minimum age requirement. Fifty years on I still shudder at the thought of hundreds of men queuing up for sex.

One night, still in Savona, I was returning to the ship ravenously hungry as usual. I saw a fast food outlet about the size of a fish and chip shop. In England at that time we in Yorkshire knew very little about Indian, Chinese or Italian cuisine. I went into the shop and made my order choosing a delicious piece of pastry covered in cheese, tomato and bits of meat. When I got back to the ship my supper created a great deal of interest and I agreed to show my shipmates where I had bought it. We all trooped back into Savona where many of the crew bought pizzas. The owner of the pizza take away was so pleased that in the following days, each time I passed, he called me in and I was handed a free pizza. Much more satisfying to a hungry lad of seventeen than standing in a bordello queue.

Some of my early visits ashore I now view as amusing, though at the time they were alarming. Whilst in a tiny West African port I had gone ashore alone one afternoon because Brian was working cargo. Loud honky tonk music was issuing forth from one of the bars, and, in fact, the whole building seemed to be vibrating and shaking. 'This,' I thought, 'is where the action is.'

I went inside and sampled some of the quite palatable local beer and some strange, strong, clear liquid out of a bottle that had twigs in the bottom. Wondering whether I might go blind or poison myself, my mind was diverted from these thoughts when I was approached by a very curvaceous girl of about my own age. We had a drink or two and then she suggested that I visit her home.

We walked about half a mile along a jungle path to a clearing containing about a dozen circular mud huts. Our arrival didn't seem to cause much of a stir as she guided me to her hut, which I noticed was very well furnished. Alarm bells should have rung at this point when, after a friendly chat, she removed all of her clothes and encouraged me to do the same. It seemed like a very good idea and I was about half way to joining her when a sudden noise alerted me to the fact that at the window, and every nook and keyhole, eyes were watching me. The locals had assembled in numbers and were all pushing and shoving for a better view of the cabaret in which I was to be a star attraction. I hurriedly got dressed and fled despite the earnest pleas of the girl; it was more than I could cope with. Fading into the distance as I ran were the raised voices of the girl and the men of the village engaged in a heated slanging match. She was not happy to be deprived of her income whilst I was extremely relieved to get back to the safety of the ship.

As I have already indicated there are times when one would rather keep quiet about one's nationality. One such occasion happened when I was in Sibenik, Yugoslavia discharging a cargo of ten thousand tons of coal dust, which I believe was a gift from the American Government.

Yugoslavia was in the serious grip of communism making it a grim place to visit, the prevailing atmosphere being one of depression, threat and secrecy. Going ashore we often noticed that two or three men would be following us and a barmaid we had befriended was suddenly no longer at work because of fears over her contact with foreign visitors. We did meet with a local family and have drinks with them but the whole event was carried out in fear and with great secrecy.

The town possessed a huge square where, at night, people simply gathered to walk up and down. Joining in this harmless activity, still shadowed by our uninvited company, we realised that the purpose of this strange nocturnal perambulation was to facilitate an encounter with the opposite sex. Eye contact led to couples peeling off and holding huddled preliminary discussions down narrow side streets.

Women worked on the docks alongside the men and were capable of very hard physical work in roles reminiscent our own Land Army girls during the Second World War. The relationship between the workers seemed good and practical jokes were commonplace. One day some men, instead of fixing the crane hooks to a tray of cargo on the back of a lorry, fastened the hooks to the lorry itself. The female crane driver, unaware of what they had done, lifted the whole lorry off the ground, much to the consternation of the driver and the great amusement of the onlookers.

There was one place in town where one could obtain an extremely good steak. This establishment was called the Hotel Kkra and, unlike me, the majority of the local people could not afford to eat there. Most weekends the hotel was frequented by military people, high-ranking officers with masses of gold braid and accompanied by elegant ladies in smart evening gowns. There was a kind of opulent banquet atmosphere.

On the evening in question two very drunken Ellerman Wilson Line apprentices arrived. Half way through a magnificent meal, these two idiots decided to blow up condoms and launch them into the air where they drifted around the splendid hall like deflating airships. Not content with this display, the two young gentlemen from Hull then crawled about beneath the tables attempting to retrieve them. Naturally the grand ladies were dismayed and alarmed at these lads scrabbling indecorously around their feet.

Brian and I feigned ignorance when faced with questions about these two clowns attempting to disguise our own nationality by adopting almost unintelligible foreign accents. We finished our meal avoiding the stares and pointing fingers of the other diners.

I found Brazil to be a vibrant, colourful country where extremes of wealth and poverty existed side by side. However, I was also to discover that although it was an exciting place to visit, it could be dangerous and needed more care than usual.

We spent several weeks on the Brazilian coast loading timber in Salvador, Rio De Janeiro, Santos and Porto Alegre. Whilst berthed in Salvador, having heard of the wonderful beaches in Brazil, I decided to go swimming one afternoon. Brian was working so I went ashore alone complete with towel and costume and found a huge, clean, very flat beach. I was rather surprised to find it totally deserted and disappointed by the absence of the legendary brown-skinned, bikini-clad girls. The beach had little gradient which indicated that when the tide changed the water would rapidly come in, so I left my bundle of clothes well up on the beach. I wondered whether the complete lack of bathers might indicate that the waters were unsafe but there seemed to be no tide or current so I enjoyed a very pleasant swim.

Coming out of the water my bundle of clothes was a speck in the distance. I started walking up the beach and noticed someone on a bike casually riding towards my clothes. I quickened my pace as an unpleasant thought passed through my mind. There was absolutely nothing on the beach except my belongings. I was certain the lad on the bike was heading for my clothes and I was going to be robbed. I began running at full speed thinking 'Well he won't find much in my wallet.' The boy on the bike never quickened his pace, as he knew he had plenty of time. In a very carefree manner he picked up all my clothes, including my shoes and towel. By now I was running like an Olympic sprinter but this brazen youth, having got what he wanted, beat a hasty retreat. Cycling on a flat, hard, sand, he soon left me far behind. I stood there swearing horribly, cursing the whole of Brazil. What could I do? I was obliged to walk barefoot in a wet costume through the town accompanied by some strange looks. All I could think about was the reception which awaited when I got back to the ship. I knew the teasing would be cruel and relentless. Could I get back onboard and into my cabin without anyone seeing me? Not a chance!

Since the days of the gauchos the knife has been the favoured fighting weapon rather than the fist. I had seen two very unpleasant incidents in bars. In the first incident a black man received several stab wounds in his backside as he tried to escape from a man with whom he had picked an argument. The second assault I witnessed was in a waterfront bar in Rio de Janeiro. I was having a quiet drink when I noticed a little, fat, smartly dressed man of middle age. He was obviously inebriated and becoming rather over familiar, verbally and physically, with the ladies. As I watched, a group of men quietly surrounded him near a wall. I saw the arm movement, but not the knife, and it was followed by an awful gasp as the men melted away and the little fat man was left clutching his stomach, blood trickling through his fingers. I quickly finished my drink and left before the law arrived.

So being aware that knives were frequently used in this country, Brian and I were perhaps rather rash on another occasion. We managed to get ashore together several times in Santos where we had found the Flying Angel Seaman's Club and had befriended some rather delectable girls. After some pretty impressive and persuasive talking, we managed to get them to meet us outside of the club the following weekend.

We took them for a drink and ended up at a real Brazilian stomp, the dance hall totally filled with young people having a great time. Now it has to be said that the local boys in any port are never too happy when they see sailors moving in on *their* girls, even though they may have never clapped eyes on them before. As Brian and I were prancing about, trying to dance, we became aware that we were on the receiving end of some fairly hard intentional bumps. Without a word being said between us, we identified the culprits. Again with eye contact only we arranged a little 'accident' for the chief perpetrator. At a suitable opportunity Brian nipped behind him and got on his hands and knees at the back of his legs just as I placed two hands on the guy's chest and gave him a hefty push. The initial results were spectacular and satisfying: he fell backwards, almost doing a backward roll. It was also a huge mistake on our part. It was not a good idea to humiliate a knife-carrying, hot-tempered Brazilian in front of his mates and, in seconds, the whole bunch of them surrounded us, brandishing knives. A violent argument broke out between them and the girls we were with. Quickly grasping what had been going on they gave the Brazilian boys a fair old tongue-lashing. They managed to get us out of the dance hall unscathed, almost acting as human shields. Unfortunately, that was the end of our promising night out.

Towards the end of my apprenticeship, I joined a brand new ship in Greenock and signed on as uncertified Third Mate. Here, I embarked on a voyage which had Sydney, Australia, as an early port of call. Once berthed, I went ashore with the Third Engineer and visited a well-known bar for a few beers. Compared to the average English pub the Australian bars were a bit disappointing. This one was no exception with its tiled walls and floors and the atmosphere of a public convenience. The Aussies were fairly free with their comments often referring to us as 'whingeing poms.' Naturally we gave as good as we got and pointed out that at least we were not the descendants of convicts. Not a sentiment which went down too well but, generally, the barracking was reasonably good natured.

I happened to notice on the bar top a large, magnificent glass ashtray. Seeing this fine example I was reminded that, not long after sailing, I had realised there wasn't a single ashtray on the whole ship. In those days almost everybody smoked except me. I had tried cigarettes but luckily found them absolutely foul. Smokers visiting my cabin were very welcome but not the ash and dog ends that they left behind. Normally an honest person, I was suddenly aware of my dire need of such a useful receptacle and decided to steal the impressive ashtray. When I thought no one was looking I surreptitiously pushed it down the top of my trousers.

Later on I needed to visit the Gents. Anyone watching my strange gait might have imagined that I was pretty desperate to relieve myself but the huge ashtray secreted in my trousers made a my normal stroll impossible.

In the Gents was a beautiful statue of a naked lady, complete with a strategically placed, hinged fig leaf. Most young, gullible, sex-starved sailors, visiting for the first time, would furtively look around before succumbing to the temptation to lift the figleaf. Unbeknown to the wretched victim, lifting the fig leaf would activate a bell in the main bar room where his return would be greeted with howls of laughter and derision.

Aware of the fig leaf I left well alone, but I was nonetheless the object of scorn when I returned to my glass of beer. The dreaded ashtray fell down my trouser leg and clanged on the tiled floor as the whole place fell silent and everyone looked at me. I was deeply embarrassed but the barman was not amused. Rushing round, he picked up the ashtray and shouted at me, 'Yes, and your bloody mate's got the other one!' Unbeknown to me, the Third Engineer had also filched an ashtray which he was then obliged to return. With our tails between our legs we were turfed out; we were not even allowed to finish our beer.

It is always a mistake to stop at the first bar outside the dock gates. I knew this, yet I still did it. We had arrived in Mombasa, Kenya in extremely hot weather, approaching 90 degrees Farenheit in the shade. I planned to have just one ice-cold beer before going further into town, feeling safe because I knew the drill: mind your own business, don't stare at anyone and don't buy any of the bar girls a drink. Very soon a girl approached me and asked me to buy her a drink. If I did so, she would take this as an indication that I was interested in her and soon she would be telling me what she had to offer. I very politely and firmly told her that I was not going to buy her a drink. Normally, that was the end of it, although another girl might try her luck. But this girl was persistent. I kept politely refusing, because I knew that if I was rude or aggressive towards her, this would give some of the local tough boys the excuse to give me a good hiding.

The girl now became aggressive and agitated and I began to think she was slightly unhinged. Eventually she walloped me on the head with an empty bottle and I noticed that her behaviour was causing a great deal of interest all round. Of equal interest, no doubt, was how I might extricate myself from this potentially very tricky situation. My natural stubbornness refused to allow me to be driven from the bar by some unhinged female.

I looked around for the meanest, toughest and biggest guy in the bar and asked him to join me. 'Do you want a job?' I asked him. 'Yes,' he said, knowing that he would be well remunerated. 'I want you to sit at that table and be my bodyguard and I'll pay you one pound.' My wage at that time was about thirty-two pounds a month so one pound was a lot of money to my temporary employee. I bought him a beer and the arrangement worked extremely well. I was left in perfect peace to enjoy my drink as on each occasion the deranged woman tried to attack me, my bodyguard drove her away.

But the excitement was not yet over. When I left the bar, I ordered a taxi to take me to the centre of town. The taxis in Mombasa were three wheelers, entirely open at the sides but covered overhead with a kind of canvas hood. As we set off up Kilindini Road, another taxi drew alongside and rammed us – a process which continued all the way into town. My driver seemed to be fully in control of the situation and so I attempted not to worry though I did wonder whether the ramming was directed at me or if it was just a dispute between rivals. I never did find out.

I had another alarming experience in a taxi in Bombay, India, now called Mumbai. I spent three years trading on the Indian coast so I had developed quite a local knowledge. Indian cities were teeming with life, people on foot, on scooters, bicycles, bullock carts, rickshaws, and in cars. Sacred cows roamed the streets making driving conditions very hazardous. I'd heard that if a car knocked someone down, the golden rule was to keep moving and report it to the nearest police station. Stopping at an accident might mean the car and its occupants being attacked by an angry mob.

On the afternoon in question, I had taken a taxi to a huge and impressive indoor market - a journey that I had done several times before so I knew what the fare should be. Arriving at the market the taxi driver attempted to substantially over-charge me. I was reasonably fluent in Hindustani so I remonstrated with him. The taxi driver was not impressed and began to tell passers-by I had refused to pay my fare and that I was trying to cheat him. Soon a very aggressive crowd surrounded the taxi and the driver whipped them into frenzy. I realised that I was in the centre of a very volatile situation. What was I going to do? In the middle of the mob I spotted a very well dressed Hindu and, above the din, managed to attract his attention and call him over. I told him that I could see that he was a very well educated and intelligent man. Flattery works wonders. I asked him if he would explain to the people that I knew exactly what the fare should be and that the taxi driver was really trying to overcharge me. The Hindu managed to get a hearing and soon a furious debate was in full swing between various parties in the crowd. As the argument grew I managed to slip away unnoticed and into the crowded market.

I was rather pleased because I had managed to extricate myself from a potentially dangerous situation. What's more, I realised later in the day that I hadn't paid any fare either.

There were many beggars on the streets of Indian cities and there was little doubt that without the generosity of people, they would starve. One remarkable beggar came to my notice in Calcutta. He was so poor that he had only a one legged stool but had perfected the practice of sleeping whilst begging. His two legs coupled with the stool's one wooden leg enabled him to balance. He then rested an elbow on the upper part of his leg, his outstretched hand holding his begging bowl. I was always fascinated to see him slumbering there. How nice it must have been to wake up and find enough money to buy himself some food.

Another blind beggar also intrigued me. From a distance I could hear him calling 'Baksheesh sahib.' As I got nearer his cry changed into the English language, recognising me as a person who had given him some money before. How did he do that, as he was obviously totally blind? I decided that there was only one possible explanation; he had developed an acute sense of hearing. He was well able to distinguish between the sounds of Indian and European footwear and could recognise people by the unique sound made by their shoes. Here was a good example of a blind person whose highly developed remaining senses compensated for his lack of sight.

I visited America many times in the 1950's and 60's. The American people gave us a warm welcome and were very kind and hospitable, but despite this friendliness, it was easier to get ashore in Russia than it was in America.

To begin with, we had to suffer a humiliating medical. The whole ship's company had to line up and drop their pants one by one. The one eyed trouser snake had to suffer a close inspection with the aid of a torch and probe to the order of 'peel.' This examination was obviously intended to reduce the spread of sexually transmitted diseases.

Secondly, at that time, the Americans were obsessed with the evils of communism. Immigration officials arrived on board with huge books, which supposedly contained the names of everyone in the world who were, or had been, members of the Communist Party. And it worked too: our Greek Second Engineer, my previous tormentor was identified, much to my delight. He was not allowed to set foot upon American soil and under huge threat if he did so.

In spite of now being streetwise and port-wise, experience taught me that America could be an unusually dangerous and violent place. In 1958 we visited New Orleans and Baton Rouge on the impressive River Mississippi to load grain. One very enjoyable experience was a trip up the river on a genuine paddle steamer but other experiences ashore were not so pleasant.

One night, I was going ashore to visit a very pretty barmaid. She had decided that I deserved copious amounts of rum and coke at heavily subsidised prices. As I was walking through a square towards the bar, a car came to a screeching halt nearby, a back door opened and a woman was flung out, rolling to a halt almost at my feet. She was covered in dust and scratches and very distressed. She claimed that she had been grabbed off the street, raped and finally ejected from the car by the three men responsible. Not wishing to become too closely involved I simply got her a drink and stayed with her until the Police arrived.

Another night I was passing a line of cars waiting to board a river ferry and for some unknown reason a woman decided she wasn't going to go any further. The husband or partner was shouting and swearing, attempting to get her back in the car. This led to quite a violent incident with the woman dodging round cars, trying to run away with the man in hot pursuit. I was soon to realise that these were not isolated happenings and this was one tough city.

A day or two later I experienced the worst visit ashore of any port in the world. I had gone ashore in the late afternoon of a beautiful sunny day and strolled through the famous areas of New Orleans such as Bourbon Street and Canal Street, very happily listening to the jazz bands in the bars.

Resuming my tour I was approached by a smartly dressed stranger who bore some resemblance to James Cagney, the actor famous for his gangster roles. Without saying a word he knocked me flat on my back. I was completely unprepared for this and naively thought that it must be a case of mistaken identity. I struggled to my feet only to receive another punch on the jaw. I am not a violent person but I do not allow anyone to hit me and I had 'turned the other cheek' by giving the stranger the benefit of the doubt. As I lay on my back for a second time I thought to myself, 'He will not do that again!' I got back to my feet and this time I was ready for him. As he swung at me for the third time I dodged his blow and knocked HIM flat on his back.

This was the start of a lengthy slugging match; although middle-aged, my assailant was certainly not short of energy. Our battle caused considerable chaos. People were diving out the way and cars were screeching to a halt as we spilled onto the road.

A policeman arrived in the form of a bear-like Irish cop. I can still picture his huge boots, like something out of a Charlie Chaplin film. Up until this point my attacker and I had not spoken a single word and I had the distinct impression that he and the policeman already knew each other. The man said that I was causing trouble and the policeman wouldn't listen to a word that I said but seized my collar and gave me what might be termed as the 'bum's rush' up the street. He obviously did not like sailors or the English and I was told in no uncertain terms to 'get back to my ship.'

Extremely angry at this unfair treatment I walked a couple of hundred yards in the right direction. All the strenuous exercise of fighting had left me famished and I couldn't resist visiting a hamburger joint. The people inside were staring at me and I realised that I looked pretty dishevelled, covered in dirt and the blood which had run down the front of my light coloured shirt. The waitress eyed me up suspiciously but as I was superficially calm she accepted my order.

In reality I was now in an evil mood, even entertaining the thought of waiting until the policeman had gone before retracing my steps to seek out the swine who had started all the trouble and gain my revenge.

The hamburger and coffee took an age to arrive as I waited with my mouth watering in hungry anticipation. Eventually I saw the waitress walking in my direction and place the food in front of me. My hand was just reaching out to pick it up when disaster struck; the policeman had returned. I had made the mistake of sitting with my back to the door so I didn't see him coming. For the second time he felt my collar, lifting me bodily off my stool and dragging me outside. 'I told you to get back to your ship' he said. He then took out his baton and beat me all the way from my ankles to my head. Realising that I was up against a totally unreasonable thug with the power of the law behind him I had no option but to return back on board. But my troubles were by no means over.

I set off in the general direction of the river. Not being familiar with my surroundings, I found that when I reached the riverside I was roughly on the same level as the water and knew this was wrong; my ship was tied up to a jetty about fifteen feet high. I looked up and down the riverbank and saw a group of large ships about a quarter of a mile away. I began to walk towards them and eventually reached the jetty only to discover that, as it towered above me, there was no obvious means of getting to the top. I considered my options but just could not face the thought of retracing my steps. I knew harbours, jetties and quaysides very well and thought there was bound to be a ladder somewhere. How else could people get in and out of small boats?

I now made another serious mistake. I decided to walk underneath the jetty thinking that I would soon reach a ladder. It was very unpleasant, even more so now darkness had fallen, and the whole structure was coated with the debris and oil left by the tidal flow. Occasionally I heard rats scampering away as I continued my fruitless search for a ladder. Eventually I reached the moored up vessels and with some relief located my own ship. I could see the gangway way above me so I tried shouting, but no one heard me. I pressed on, still sure that I would come across a ladder going up to the top. Soon I came across a rusty wire hanging from the top of the jetty over the fast flowing river but it was beyond my reach. 'Was it tied fast up there?' I wondered. I was now filthy, tired and desperate. Desperation made me reckless and I decided to jump for the wire. I knew that if it was not made fast I would plunge into the river with the wire on top of me. Even so, I was fairly confident that I would be able to get out of the water.

I jumped for the wire and hung on as I wildly swung about. Great relief! It held. It was no mean feat climbing up that rusty wire and, when I reached the top, put one arm over the timber rail and then the other. I was resting there, gathering up energy for the final pull over the rail, when I noticed a man in uniform standing about two feet in front of me. This part of the jetty was deserted and I realised the man was a Night Watchman. He was obviously miles away in thought, whistling aimlessly as he looked out over the river. 'This man is going to get a shock,' I thought. 'Now how am I going to do this?' I decided to be very English and so I announced my presence by simply saying 'Good Evening, sir.' He was extremely startled and looked at me in horror then ran off at high speed. What I could not know was that he was running to a telephone.

I completed my climb and examined myself. My suit was ruined and I had added oil and rust to the dust and blood. I was trying to dust myself down and thinking my problems were over when a police car came screaming down the jetty. Please God, don't let it be the same policeman that I've already met today- but I need not have worried. Inside the car were two policemen and the Night Watchman and I was unceremoniously bundled into the back and told not to move. For some strange reason the Night Watchman was convinced that somebody else must be down there underneath the jetty. He just could not bring himself to believe that I was down there alone. He produced a rope ladder and the two overweight and rather unfit policemen disappeared over the edge of the jetty to look for the non-existent person.

When the two policemen returned they were covered in oil and dirt and not in good humour. They plainly felt I was to blame and I felt certain that I was destined to be locked up for the night. The policemen, however, were still convinced that someone was under the jetty and I was taken back to my ship where the policemen insisted on a roll call. The Captain, who was asleep, was not at all happy to be disturbed in order to carry out a pointless roll call with half the crew still ashore. At last I was left alone and I soon found the safety of my bunk.

The next morning I was by no means Mr. Popular as the crew members who had been disturbed by the Captain and the two policemen greeted me with a considerable verbal battering. I was bruised from head to toe, mainly from the policeman's baton and unable to tell anyone my side of the story because I had a kind of lockjaw from the first two punches I had received. I resolved never to go ashore again as I thought the place was just too dangerous.

My resolution was very short-lived. After three days the pretty barmaid sent me a message asking why I hadn't been to see her. The thought of free rum and coke and pleasant surroundings was more than I could resist.

A week later we sailed further up the River Mississippi to a port called Baton Rouge. We had a very pleasant stay in Baton Rouge apart from a drunken dispute on board ship which will be further explored later in these reminiscences. What was even more memorable and shocking was what happened to a young boy on a Swedish ship moored nearby.

The lad was seventeen years old and already a huge six footer. He had gone ashore, had far too much to drink and, as is often the case, turned very aggressive. He had broken a bottle and was using the jagged remains to threaten the barman. The barman's response was to produce a shotgun and summarily shoot him dead. A broken bottle can be a very dangerous and fearsome weapon and some would say he got what he deserved, but a barman or landlord in most countries would have been able to deal with that situation without anyone getting hurt. The barman was not locked up and faced no charges, merely suspended for a few days until the Swedish ship sailed. The local police, aware that the Swedish crew were very upset, moved the barman away temporarily for his own safety. As for me, I had often considered emigrating to America but news of this incident convinced me that this was not a place in which I could live.

Chapter 9

First Aid- Last Aid

As I mentioned in a previous chapter there were no doctors on the majority of merchant ships. As a gesture towards the risk this might imply, both Third Mate and Second Mate were usually trained first aiders and had to deal with all the medical problems. Although I sustained a few minor injuries at different times, a cracked bone in my elbow, a gashed forehead and a broken wrist, fortunately, I was able to receive hospital treatment on each occasion.

The broken wrist was entirely my own fault, the result of some foolish behaviour when, on one occasion, I was drinking in the Cricket Club in Colombo, Sri Lanka. The European expatriates in the club were a hard drinking bunch and on the evening in question, a game of cricket was being played inside the bar with a real cricket ball. Glasses, mirrors and bottles were being smashed frequently and I found myself cowering on my stool wondering when the hard ball was going to hit me on the head. Miraculously no one was hurt. Considerable damage having been done, the drunken revellers turned to throwing darts, a pastime which ceased only when all of the darts were stuck in the ceiling. A debate ensued about how these might be rescued and some bright spark suddenly piped up with, 'Don't worry, John will get them down for you. He's good at climbing.' This was true in that I was always quite happy to climb the mast on board ship if any jobs needed doing up there. However, on this occasion, alcohol was fuelling my bravado. Starting on a chair and then using a dado rail I was able to reach up to the exposed roof beams. Once up there I could successfully retrieve most of the darts. Unfortunately on my descent a plaster ridge gave way and down I came. To save falling flat on my back I put my arms behind me and landed rather heavily. The following day, now fully sober and in considerable pain, I realised my wrist was broken. Despite hospital treatment my right wrist has never fully recovered to this day.

Luckily, death at sea is very rare. Seamen are usually healthy from the strenuous physical activity which is part and parcel of their daily routine and the injuries they sustain are mostly self-inflicted. However, being at sea did not make one immune from sad or unpredictable events.

Henry was a barrel-chested Able Seaman, twenty-eight years of age and looking more like a jolly farmhand than a sailor. With his Irish charm and cheerfulness he was fun to know and I well remember chatting to him late one afternoon as we sailed along in the Gulf of Oman. He was in a happy, relaxed mood and I enjoyed our conversation. To the bemused shock of everyone on board he was found dead in his bunk at three forty-five the following morning. The standby man was calling him for the four to eight watch and failed to rouse him. We had no idea what had caused his death but, heading for the Persian Gulf as we were, the temperature was not dropping below ninety degrees Fahrenheit in the shade and the Captain had little option but to arrange a quick sea burial.

None of the sailors would agree to sew up poor Henry in canvas. In any case, as most of the crew had experience only of tankers, they had none of the skills needed to handle canvas. The Captain told the Chief Officer to see to it, and the Chief Officer told the Second and Third Mate to find someone to do it. Eventually Harry and I, the youngest lads on the ship, were ordered to sew him up with the promise of a bottle of rum after the job was done.

Poor Henry was duly delivered to us in a dark and dingy tween deck. We obtained some heavy pieces of iron and secured these in a makeshift shroud. Next we sewed him up in a clean white sheet and finally, sadly, in canvas. We completed the job in total silence.

The sailors rigged up a platform on deck made up of a well-greased board and a forty-gallon drum. One end of the board was resting on the ship's rail, the other end on the drum. The ship was stopped for Henry's sea burial as the entire ship's company assembled on the main deck. Henry was carried out and placed on the board where he was covered with a brand new Red Ensign. The Chief Officer stationed Harry and me at the end of the board with the strict instruction that we should not lose the flag overboard.

A great gloom settled over us all as the Captain read the burial service. When he said solemnly 'We commit this body to the deep,' Harry and I lifted the board, trying to keep hold of the flag at the same time.

Henry refused to move. We lifted the greased board higher but he wouldn't budge. We tried shaking the board but that didn't work either. Holding the board up with my left hand, I let go of the flag and put my right hand on the top of Henry's head. At this point the Chief Officer rushed forward and whispered in my ear, 'Don't lose the Ensign John!' I was furious. 'Is that all he can think about at a time like this?' I thought. I pushed hard on Henry's head. I could feel the skin of his scalp move underneath my hand, the recollection of which made me shudder for months afterwards.

My push did the trick and Henry slid off and fell with a huge splash into the ocean. But then, instead of sinking, he floated around. Had we included enough iron? We waited for a few minutes until, with great relief, we saw him slide feet first into the depths before we all shuffled dejectedly off to our cabins. The sound of the telegraph bells shattered the silence as someone rang 'Full Ahead Engines' on the Bridge. Harry and I simply opened our bottle rum.

The Captain wrote a beautiful letter to Harry's parents in Ireland explaining what had happened. The Second Mate enclosed a chart with a cross marked on it, showing exactly where we buried him.

'You'd put your p***k where I wouldn't put my walking stick,' was the drawling, scornful comment from Captain Mad Farris. This unsympathetic retort was aimed at some sorry looking sailors who had discovered that they had left port with more than a hangover. The Captain, as I recall, didn't own a walking stick but the comment was graphically appropriate. Sexually transmitted diseases were an occupational hazard and time spent in foreign ports always had the potential for providing foolhardy crew members with a leaving present.

The Second Mate and I often had to deal with sexually transmitted diseases, a task which didn't exactly fill us with 'joie de vivre.' On one occasion I was asked to escort an Arab fireman to a hospital for treatment having contracted what was colloquially known as 'a dose of the clap.' The hospital, situated in Santos, Brazil, was a magnificent, pristine place that gave every impression of being a well-run establishment. As we waited to be attended to, a well-dressed lady stopped to talk to us. I came to the conclusion that she was a well-meaning volunteer visitor, her role being to chat to the patients. She soon lost interest in me when she realised that I was not ill but the fireman, despite his pleasant nature, had no wish to talk about his ailment. She was determined to find out what was wrong with him and the fireman showed every sign of discomfort as he evaded her inquiries. I really felt sorry for him but there was little I could do as he eventually blurted out, 'I sick with bad woman.' The reaction from the lady was one of revulsion as she suddenly realised what had brought him here and she left us abruptly, glancing back only once with a look of disapproval and distaste.

Our involvement with the sick sometimes required a hands-on approach. We signed on a Cook who was being treated for Syphilis, a very serious venereal disease. He came with medical notes, drugs and instructions for their administration. The Second Mate and I, as qualified first-aiders, were delegated to continue his treatment. Despite the fact that we were both very inexperienced, we had to give the man an injection every day.

This pre-dated the availability of disposable hypodermic needles and we searched our tiny hospital only to find some needles that looked more suited to an elephant or rhinoceros. Neither of us had ever given an injection before but we knew what to do in theory and the procedure seemed self-evident. The bluntness of our needles, the leathery hide of the cook or the lack of the cool gentle hands of a sympathetic nurse together conspired to make this process a thoroughly memorable and painful experience for him.

News spread around the ship that we had a cook who was being treated for Syphilis. The thought of him kneading dough or cutting up raw meat was more than we could bear and so it was not long before a delegation visited the Captain to voice our concerns. The Captain assured us that the disease could not be transmitted through food, a statement which convinced no-one and the grumbling continued. Eventually the Captain had to invite a doctor on board to talk to us. He addressed the whole ship's company and insisted that this dreadful disease could not be passed on through food. We had no option but to accept what he had told us but it would be impossible to say that we ate our food with any enthusiasm.

As one of the recognised first-aiders I had to deal with a wide variety of minor accidents. One night I was called out to give first aid to an Asian who had fallen out of a top bunk whilst asleep. I quickly ascertained the extent of his injuries; there were a number of obvious lacerations but I also noted that he appeared semi conscious and suffering from shock. This was beyond my limited expertise. Luckily we were docked in Liverpool at the time and an ambulance was called and he was admitted to hospital. In the way of these things the ship sailed before he was well enough to return.

Sometimes mistakes were made. A fireman fell in the engine room and was unable to get up again. I collected my first aid bag and went to examine him. No bones were broken but he had a very nasty gash on his knee. I decided that I would clean it thoroughly before applying a dressing. Leaving my first aid bag on the metal deck, I told the Fourth Engineer that I was going to get a basin of warm water.

When I returned the poor fireman had either fainted or was unconscious. There was a strong smell of Dettol. 'What happened?' I asked.

'Well,' said the Fourth Engineer, 'I thought I would clean him up for you. I just put some Dettol on cotton wool and started to clean his wound. He let out a horrible scream and passed out.'

'You did what?' I yelled. 'Did you dilute it first?'

'Well no, I didn't know I had to.' He had actually soaked the man's open wound with neat Dettol. Little wonder he had passed out.

Luckily, most accidents occurred in port, which was a good thing because we could obtain proper medical help. One night I was on duty in New Orleans. We were not working cargo so it was an easy job and I was lurking around in the shadows as the sailors returned, staggering drunk. I was just keeping an eye on them in case anyone fell in the river; it was not uncommon for a man to fall between the ship and the jetty.

When the sailors had tottered off to their quarters, I noticed a lone figure stumbling towards the gangway. I realised that it was Rodney the Second Mate, always something of a colourful character. I was puzzled by what seemed to be a dark stripe starting at his nose and continuing down his clothes. When he arrived on board, I realised that it was blood. Rodney, as was often the case, was befuddled with drink but managed to explain that he had tripped over the first rail of a railway line. The bridge of his nose had hit the second rail as he fell flat on his face. I cleaned him up and realised that he needed hospital treatment as bits of bone were clearly visible. However, Rodney did not want to go to the hospital even though I was adamant he should. In desperation I said, 'Well what can I do with your nose? We can't leave it with bits of bone sticking out.'

'Well, just bloody well re-shape it as best you can.'

So I did. I think the alcohol he had consumed must have numbed the pain because he never complained.

The next morning, he had two black eyes as well as a swollen and battered nose, not to mention a hangover. He never sought any further treatment and in time his injury healed over completely and he viewed the whole incident as a joke.

Sadly, another death occurred, but this time in port. I was working on an Asian crew ship and we were berthed in Madras, India. During lunch, one of the stewards, an elderly Indian, felt ill and went to lie down on his bunk. Fifteen minutes later he was dead. Our agent informed the local authorities and we were told that someone would come to collect the body. Two hours later, a very smart Indian policeman arrived with a flat-backed bullock cart.

It is a very strange thing that when an unpleasant job has to be done, everyone suddenly disappears. The Captain, Chief Officer, and the Second Mate had all mysteriously vanished but I couldn't escape because I was on cargo-work duty. I press-ganged a couple of apprentices and obtained a special stretcher. Wrapping the dead man in a clean white sheet, we secured him to the stretcher. The careful process of carrying him up the stairs, along the deck and down the gangway was far from easy.

Once on the dockside we laid him on the bullock cart and endeavoured to recover our stretcher. It was then that I had a bit of a disagreement with the policeman who insisted that we should keep the sheet in which we had wrapped the body. I remonstrated at length with him, even suggesting it was a gift, but the wretched official insisted we remove the sheet. Luckily the poor deceased was still in his working clothes and the cart creaked off with the poor man flat on his back, eyes wide open staring at the bright sky. I was very sad and angry to see him depart this way. Surely he could have been treated with a little more dignity.

Finally, a dreadful accident which almost killed a man. Luckily for him, we were in the port of Bombay working cargo. No one really knew how the accident happened, but it is probable that Robert, the Fourth Engineer was sleepwalking at the time. In his sleep state he was probably attempting to go on duty and in doing so fell from the top of the engine room, some thirty to forty feet, all the way to the bottom. His body actually broke a wrought iron gate valve as he bounced off various obstacles on his journey downwards.

When he was discovered it was obvious that he had terrible head injuries. Being almost impossible to carry him out of the engine room we strapped him in a special stretcher and hauled him out vertically with a stout rope. Careful hands guided him past the many obstructions.

An ambulance was already waiting by the time we got him on deck. Mad Farris, the eccentric Captain was very upset to see a young man so severely injured. He instructed me to accompany Robert in the ambulance and told me to 'Stay with him at all times. Make sure he gets proper medical treatment.'

In the ambulance I had an opportunity to have a good look at the unconscious Robert. He was bleeding from his ears, nose and mouth as well as having fits. The rest of his body appeared unscathed but I knew that his chances of survival were slim.

Upon arrival at a large hospital Robert was immediately taken to the casualty department. I never left his side. Some nurses who by their nun's dress appeared to be from some religious order promptly examined him. They looked at each other and shook their heads silently. At this point a doctor hadn't seen him.

Some orderlies put him on a trolley and took him to a ward where I assumed that he would receive some treatment. By now his fits were so severe that he was tied to a bed with bandages. Suddenly, the orderlies vanished and I was left there sitting with him. After a short while it dawned upon me that he was not going to get any treatment and that he had been left there to die.

The ward had a scattering of other patients but there were no doctors or nurses to be seen. I was pacing up and down wondering what to do when along came a very well dressed lady. I asked her if she was a doctor. Speaking in very good English she told me that she was an Almoner: a social worker in the hospital. I was now very angry as my poor shipmate had not received any treatment whatsoever and was obviously fighting for his life. I politely asked if she could take me to the doctor in charge of the hospital, which she did.

Luckily, I was dressed in full uniform, complete with hat, and well aware of the effect it had on people. I'm not sure whether to be ashamed or proud of what I did next. I gave the doctor the most severe dressing down he had ever experienced in his life. I ranted and raved like a lunatic. I criticised his nurses, his staff and the hospital. Finally I produced a pen and notebook and told him that I had recorded the times and a diary of events since we arrived. 'If my shipmate doesn't get some treatment soon,' I told him, 'there will be hell to pay.'

My notebook was actually blank but the bluff worked: The top doctor was galvanised into action. Very soon doctors surrounded Robert and he was examined, given injections and rushed off to theatre. I stayed with him right to the theatre door. At this point I thought 'I can't do any more now,' so I returned to the ship.

A solemn atmosphere greeted me as I stepped on board. I received a few sympathetic comments, which I didn't understand at the time as I hurried to report to the Captain. Before I could deliver my news the Captain said sadly, 'Well, you did your best.'

'What do you mean?' I enquired. 'He's just gone into theatre.'

It turned out that the Captain had been informed about an hour previously that Robert was dead. I assured him that this was not the case and I had left him alive only a few minutes previously.

Robert survived an operation on his fractured skull and, skilfully, they had managed to repair the brain damage. We sailed the following day wondering just how well he would recover.

Three months later we had our answer. When we sailed into London, Robert was standing on the quayside as we moored up. We were all extremely pleased to learn that he had made a complete recovery. However, his medical fitness had been withdrawn by the authorities and, sadly, his sea-going days had been brought to an end.

Chapter 10

Yo Ho Ho and a Bottle of Rum

"**R**um, bum and baccy" were the old sailing ship crew's delights - or so legend would have you believe. Happily, the only one I had a leaning for was rum and soon learned that drinking was part of a sailor's life; anyone who was teetotal hardly had a friend on board the ship. The aim of many of today's youngsters seems to be to get drunk as fast as possible, in sharp contrast to our practice as sailors which was to attempt to hold our drink and stay in control. To go on watch drunk was considered a crime; men's lives could be put at risk. We studied our drink and knew instinctively what would make us ill, morose or merry and always turned out for work no matter how savage the hangover. Most of my drinking activities were very happy occasions though I have many recollections of others which nowadays would certainly be considered as alcohol abuse.

Most drinking occurred in port, in cabins and, of course, in bars ashore. The able seamen, often a closely knit group, usually went ashore together and their return usually heralded a great deal of falling about, incoherent conversation, laughter and, sometimes, fighting. I remember one huge sailor who decided he wanted to punch me. Each time he swung at me, I ducked and he would fall flat on the deck. At this he laughed uproariously, stood up, and had another attempt. Through incidents like this I became quite expert at handling drunken sailors often employing patience, friendliness or a cigarette as a means of coaxing them into their bunks.

In Dunkirk I witnessed an absolutely heart-stopping incident. We had moored up in a very unusual way with great balks of timber holding the ship off the quayside. This enabled large barges to slide between the ship and the quay so that cargo could be discharged directly into them. On the night in question there were no barges in attendance and it was about eleven p.m. that nine sailors returned, reeling drunk. I was watching them from a discreet vantage point as they approached the stern of the ship, coming to an unsteady halt near one of the balks of timber which was level with their accommodation. With horror I realised what they were thinking – that it would be much quicker to board the ship across the balk of timber rather than use the gangway which was amidships.

It is not difficult to imagine the scene. The balk of wood was twelve inches wide, fifteen feet long and secured about twelve feet above the water and this drunken assembly of individuals was clearly preparing to attempt a harrowing tightrope walk to the ship's rail. My attempts to plead with them not to do it were to no avail so I hurriedly seized lifebelts and a heaving line. By now, other crew members had arrived to watch this dangerous spectacle. The first seaman ventured across, sometimes teetering on one leg, arms waving in the air he made it safely to the ship. Strangely, this seemed to give courage to the rest of them as, one by one, they struggled after him, some on hands and knees. We held our breath until the last, a Junior Ordinary Seaman, tumbled over the ship's rail onto the deck. To our tremendous relief, perhaps thanks to some unseen guiding hand, not one fell in the water.

This kind of drunken incident occurred in a variety of forms and I recall another occasion when we were anchored off a West African port. There was quite a swell running so boarding or disembarking was quite tricky for even the most experienced of us. Singing and shouting alerted us to the arrival of a boatload of drunken sailors. How were we going to get them on board safely? The small motorboat was rising and falling about eight feet alongside the ship and climbing a pilot ladder is not easy at the best of times. If a man fell off the ladder backwards into the boat he would be badly injured. If he fell into the water it would be difficult to retrieve him.

The first thing we did was to pull up the pilot ladder temporarily, an action which drew howls of protest. We then prepared a lifeline with a large loop on the end, something which in their drunken state they were unwilling to use. However, we gave them a simple choice – to put the loop over their head and underneath their armpits if they expected us to help them up the pilot ladder, or be marooned on the motorboat.

In this way we got them back onboard one by one, but not without mishap. Several of them fell off the ladder, which they thought hugely funny. This gave them the idea of turning it into a game. They started jumping off the ladder deliberately, launching themselves into space and swinging along the ship's side, accompanied by howls of laughter. For the men on deck it was far from amusing, having to bear the full weight of a sailor on the end of the lifeline as they were dragged up the ship's side and dumped unsympathetically onto the deck.

Our policy in situations such as this was always to get each individual on board safely, as drunken sailors have an unfortunate habit of falling into the dock. It is not unknown for a body to float to the surface when a ship sets sail, the sad post script to a drunken spree ashore.

You may think, reading this book, that violence was commonplace when, in actual fact, it was quite rare and usually associated with drink.

There are no policemen on merchant ships, nor a even cell in which to lock someone up. Most of the ships on which I served had one pair of handcuffs, but I never saw them used. The Captain was the law. He had the authority to fine members of his crew small amounts of money, but his greatest power was to make an entry in a Seaman's Discharge Book which could end his career in the Merchant Navy. Serious troublemakers could therefore be easily weeded out. One eccentric Skipper I sailed with must have held a license for a small firearm as he used to carry out target practice on the boat deck. I never saw anything like a mutiny but was well aware that a Captain, faced with this prospect, would not hesitate to call upon the support of a warship.

I did witness a few minor drunken attacks on officers. On one trampship where I felt particularly threatened, I had perfected an escape route through my porthole onto the main deck – a feat which took less than 3 seconds.

Despite the fact that ships are intrinsically noisy I was always able to sleep soundly but with one ear listening, as you might say. Thus if the engines stopped at sea I would wake instantly and the same would happen if someone was approaching my cabin door. The advantage of being quickly awake is well illustrated by what befell a Chief Officer I served with who was roused by a number of drunken sailors approaching his cabin door. Having no means of escape, he jumped out of bed and hid in his wardrobe. Intoxicated people do strange things, and these intruders were no exception. Without even switching on his cabin light they gave his bunk a damn good thrashing, too drunk even to notice the absence of his sleeping form. Mission accomplished, or so they assumed, they staggered off to their own quarters. The Chief merely locked his door and returned to his bunk.

The following morning he made sure that the Bosun had them all out on deck working at eight a.m. and made a point of visiting each of the culprits, now suffering head throbbing hangovers. He enquired after their well-being, told them how good he was feeling and how great it was to be alive. The puzzled, quizzical looks with which they responded pleased him enormously. Did they even remember the happenings of the night before? We never found out.

I was involved in an extremely unpleasant incident in Botany Bay, Australia. We had discharged our cargo of crude oil and we were ready to return to sea. Unfortunately all the Able Seamen were still ashore, well overdue, and our berth was needed for another vessel. We had little option but to let go of the moorings and anchor out in the bay. The Old Man was absolutely furious and decided on a drastic course of action. He obtained each man's Seaman's Discharge Book and made a 'D.R' entry. Entries were usually limited to one of three abbreviations: 'Ex.' (Excellent), 'V.g.' (Very good) or 'D.R' (Decline to Report). One D.R would simply make it difficult to get another job whilst three D.R's would result in dismissal from the Merchant Navy.

The sailors returned by boat in dribs and drabs, much the worse for drink. As they climbed on board, the Captain threw their discharge books at their feet. Sullenly, they picked them up, looked inside and ambled off. One young seaman however, became very aggressive when he saw his D.R entry and launched a physical attack upon the Captain. Harry, the other apprentice, and I together with the Chief Engineer immediately moved in to protect him. To our surprise the Captain, an elderly unfit man, told us to move aside saying, 'Let him come if he wants to have a go.'

There now began a real slugging match. To our astonishment it was not the Captain who needed protection but the seaman. He took a savage beating which left him sprawled semi-conscious on the deck. The Captain now told Harry and I to fetch the log line - about six hundred feet of plaited hemp usually used for streaming the log at sea. We had no idea why he wanted the rope, but when we returned the Captain said, 'John, help me tie him up.'

I was horrified and said, 'No Sir, I'll put the handcuffs on him but I won't tie him up with rope.'

'Right then Harry, you help me tie him up.'

'No Sir. I won't tie him up with rope either.' We were both very worried as we were unsure of the implications of refusing an order from the Captain.

'Well get the bloody handcuffs then!' he said.

Harry and I went to the ship's office and after a rapid search found the handcuffs locked and without a key. We returned with these useless items and gave them to a still very irate Captain. 'Well I'll bloody tie him up myself then,' he said. The three of us watched helplessly as the Captain tied the poor man up. Incredibly, he used the whole length of the rope, winding it round and round his body until only his head was visible. We were then ordered to carry the badly beaten sailor to the ship's hospital where the Chief Steward was instructed to lock him in. Then, as if nothing had happened, our gallant Captain went for dinner.

I was really troubled by what had happened. The seaman certainly should not have attacked the Captain, but then it was barbaric and inhuman to tie him up with rope. He needed first aid. I had noticed that one of his

123

eyes had what looked like a serious injury and, very proud of being British, decided this just wasn't fair play. To hell with the consequences I thought, I am going to untie him. I went to the Chief Steward and asked him for the hospital key. At first he refused. 'Don't worry,' I told him, 'I'm just going to give the poor chap a cup of tea.'

'Well make sure you lock him in again and don't tell the Captain that I've given you the key'.

I let myself in and unwound the rope until his arms were free. I gave him a cup of tea and told him that I thought he was a bloody fool. I opened a porthole and looked knowingly at him. He understood. I locked him in again and returned the key to the Chief Steward. As far as I know, my secret visit to the hospital was never discovered.

The Captain finished his meal just in time to see the seaman run along the deck and clamber into the immigration boat which was still alongside. This was rather ironic because the very officials who were responsible for making sure all the crew were on board now had a deserter on their hands. They tried very hard to persuade him to climb back on board but he was absolutely adamant. The Captain made no efforts whatsoever to get him back and the last we saw and heard of our troublesome seaman was a stream of foul-mouthed abuse directed at our Skipper as the small motor-boat sailed away. I've often wondered what became of him.

You might have got the impression that the Able Seamen were responsible for all the heavy drinking and violence but it wasn't so. Drinking, usually in port was common in all ranks. In fact, it could be claimed the higher the rank, the greater the imbibing. Two officers come to mind, Rodney and Charles, who together joined a trampship where I was the uncertified Third Officer. It has to be said that some trampship officers were not the 'best pick of the bunch' and were there because they could not hold down regular posts in more reputable companies.

Rodney claimed that he was a Lieutenant Commander R.N.R (Retd). He joined the ship in London as Second Officer in a very smart uniform complete with ceremonial sword. The sword raised eyebrows amongst hard bitten trampship men, as you might expect. He was cheerful and well spoken but very condescending and dismissive of mortals he considered to be beneath his station. Certainly able to navigate and keep watch whilst at sea, in port he knew nothing about cargowork and was almost useless. However, I supposed this was to be expected if he truly was ex Royal Navy.

Charles also joined the ship in London. He was in his fifties, held a Master Mariner's Certificate and signed on as Chief Officer. A large, well educated man whose bearing commanded respect, he clearly liked his uniform, and wore it well. He was obviously a very experienced seaman both at sea and in port, though he expected me to do all of the cargo work. Charles was a bachelor, the author of numerous books and fluent in Spanish but, being a man of high morals, disapproved of anyone mixing with ladies of 'ill repute.'

Charles and Rodney had one thing in common - they both drank like fish. They never touched a drop at sea but once in port they went into non-stop drinking mode.

The Captain was a teetotal Welshman whose initial response was to keep dropping in on their drinking parties, hoping he might discourage them. Much of their serious drinking took place whilst we were working cargo. The ship had numerous empty cabins, offices and storerooms to which Charles and the Captain had a pass key. To hide from him, Rodney and Charles began to use some of these empty rooms and invented special names for them for my benefit. Thus at the beginning of the day I would be told rather haughtily, 'Oh John, we're in the Green Room today.' Being responsible for all the cargo work, I had to know where Charles was in order to liaise with him.

Each day the Captain would go looking for them. He must have guessed that I knew where they were but never compromised me by asking. Although he inevitably found them, he never delivered a reprimand. Once discovered they would promptly move to another drinking den. 'Oh John, we've moved to the Pink Room.'

They consumed vast quantities of tinned beer but never lost control, though its effect upon Rodney was to turn him a kind of reddish purple colour. Charles was always on top of the cargo work situation so the loading and discharging always proceeded smoothly. However, this was by dint of the fact that I was doing all the work.

This mad, bizarre way of working all fell apart in Baton Rouge, Louisiana, America. To begin with the wireless operator tried to kill Rodney. Sparks was a very powerfully built man from a working class background, very blunt and entirely devoid of a sense of humour. He hated Rodney with a passion, along with his accent, superior manner and immaculate uniform. Rodney, on the other hand, barely noticed Sparks' existence.

My cabin was next door to Rodney's and when I lay down in my bunk, my head would only be a few inches away from his. One night I inexplicably woke up in the early hours of the morning to hear a muffled voice next door. Unknown to me, Sparks had been drinking heavily and descended into a morose and evil mood. In his befuddled state of mind he must have decided to vent his anger on Rodney.

As my consciousness sharpened the muffled voice next door seemed to be saying, 'I am going to kill you.' I leapt out of my bunk and ran round to Rodney's cabin. His door was open and, sure enough, Sparks had him pinned on his back in his bunk and was strangling him. 'Jesus, Sparks!' I shouted, 'You'll kill him!' Rodney was already blue in the face with his eyes bulging but my appearance must somehow have jogged Sparks into the realisation of the enormity of what he was doing. Without a word he released Rodney, turned on his heel, and promptly left the room.

A frightened and gasping Rodney gulped his gratitude and then he too fled the cabin in order to wake up the Captain and tell him that Sparks had tried to kill him. The Captain was extremely annoyed to be disturbed for he had no love for the Second Mate. He did however visit Sparks' cabin to find him sitting quietly, having by now descended into a boozer's gloom. This prompted the Captain to give Rodney a piece of his mind. 'Fighting mad? What are you ranting about? Lock your cabin door and go to sleep!'

This reaction could have afforded Rodney little comfort and, returning to my bunk, it was some considerable time before I was able to resume my disturbed slumbers.

It was not going to be a happy week for Rodney as, a few days later, Charles issued a strange order. He told the Bosun that no women were to be allowed on the ship and, to enforce his ruling, an Able Seaman was going to be posted on the gangway every night. I was certainly puzzled by this restriction but then Charles was a very moral man and had little regard for ladies of doubtful repute.

Rodney was the first to run foul of Charles' unreasonable ruling. When an Able Seaman tried to prevent Rodney from bringing a young lady on board, his pompous response was something to the effect of 'Don't be a fool, get out of the way man!' and pushed past him. The Able Seaman promptly told the Bosun what had happened, who in turn informed the Chief Officer.

Charles decided to enforce his ruling himself and promptly knocked on Rodney's cabin door where a brief conversation took place. The door was then slammed shut and locked. It was at this point that I woke up and tried to assess what was going on. Charles was livid and went to get his pass key since Rodney refused to open his door. A violent argument ensued culminating with Rodney grabbing the pass key, Charles being ejected into the alleyway and the door locked again.Charles now made a serious error of judgement. He instructed the Bosun and two able seamen to break down Rodney's cabin door. They needed no second bidding as Rodney was no favourite of theirs either. The door duly broken down, Charles rushed in and a rather pathetic fight commenced.

Up until this point I had been a rather helpless observer wondering what, if anything, I could do. The girl was naked on the bed, cowering with fright whilst the three seamen were enjoying the whole spectacle. I was completely sober and very angry with my two senior officers. First I tactfully suggested to the Bosun, a Glaswegian who could be quite dangerous, that he was no longer required. Though he carried a knife and single-handedly could terrorise all the sailors, he accepted my authority and withdrew when I asked him to. I then told the girl to leave the ship. She didn't bother getting dressed but simply grabbed her clothes and ran. I now turned my attention to my two fighting colleagues, forcing them apart and giving them an almighty telling off. By the time I had finished they were both hanging their heads in shame. Finally I told Charles, 'Go to your cabin. Lock the door and go to sleep.' Rodney made some mumbled attempt to thank me. 'Don't thank me,' I shouted, 'I think you're a bloody disgrace. Go to sleep.' Peace was restored, but sadly the dispute continued the next day when Rodney tried once more to bring his lady friend on board and Charles tried an even more ridiculous way of asserting his authority. This time he called the Police in an attempt to get Rodney arrested. Luckily, the American cop was a very patient and experienced man. 'Aw, c'mon Chief, you can't have your own Second Officer arrested,' he said. Pursuing this eminently sensible line he managed to persuade Charles to change his mind.

That was the end of their drinking antics; they barely spoke to each other again. As far as I am aware all of these events took place without the Captain knowing anything whatsoever about them. Miraculously, Rodney survived until the end of the trip but Charles was sacked a few weeks later in Hamburg. His heavy drinking continued as did his reliance on me for cargo work.

One day I joined him for a drink in a bar on the docks called Bills Bar. The bar was full of huge German dockers eating their sandwiches and drinking beer. Charles was in a depressed mood staring disconsolately into his glass of beer haunted perhaps by memories of the Second World War. Suddenly, without any preamble, he stood on his chair, turned around and shouted 'The only good Germans are dead bastards.' The place fell totally silent. About forty huge, tough looking Germans stared hard at us and I was immediately terrified as I anticipated the physical onslaught which would surely follow. The total silence seemed to last for forever but it was probably only seconds and to my intense relief and surprise the Germans elected to resume their eating, drinking and talking. Charles seemed very disappointed that his outburst had not achieved the desired effect. He sat down dejectedly and continued staring into his beer as I decided it was high time I returned to the ship.

Charles was now a lone drinker and though he still kept a close eye on cargo work, he did so only through me. A few days after we had arrived in Hamburg, the Company's Marine Superintendent unexpectedly arrived on board and immediately based himself in the ship's office which had been provided with a telephone. He must have soon become aware that Charles was missing and I alone was supervising the unloading of the cargo as Rodney only made the occasional walk around the decks. This usually ended with some inane remark to me along the lines of 'Good man. Carry on.' This was because he didn't have a clue about what was going on.

Charles, who was still drinking in Bills Bar, had made arrangements to ring me at three p.m. so that I could give him an update on the cargo situation. I went to the ship's office at about five to three to find the Marine Superintendent sitting next to the phone. Rather alarmed, I thought that this situation had the potential to prove difficult. The phone rang promptly at three o clock and I moved in quickly to answer it. 'I'll answer it thank you Third Mate,' said the Marine Super taking the phone and leaving me a helpless listener.

'Hello......No I'm afraid he's not available at the moment. Who is this speaking? Oh, it's the Chief Officer. Where are you please? Oh you're in Bills Bar. Well, this is your Marine Superintendent speaking. I want you to report back on board immediately.'

Charles had been led like a lamb to the slaughter. Arriving back on board Charles was promptly dismissed and told to pack his bags; within an hour he was down the gangway and on his way back to England. I didn't even get the opportunity to say goodbye to him. Obviously, the Captain had briefed the Marine Superintendent on Charles' failings as Chief Officer, hence his rapid dismissal though neither of them said a single word to me about Charles' demise.

A few weeks later I signed off the ship to return to Boulevard Nautical College, Hull to study for a Second Mate's certificate. I had difficulty getting off the ship as the Captain continually delayed signing me off the 'Ship's Articles' and I was being pressurised to do another trip. Finally, in desperation, I rang my union and an official from the 'Merchant Navy and Airline Officers Association' visited the ship and I was released the following day. I thought that this marked the end of my days on trampships and tankers but that did not prove to be the case.

Very heavy drinking over a long period of time can lead to a condition known as 'Delirium Tremens' commonly known as the D.T.'s among sailors. Sufferers can experience hallucinations and terrifying delusions.

The same skipper who was obviously drinking at the time of the English Channel distress call continued drinking heavily for many months. No one ever saw him drinking, but the Chief Steward confided that he was drinking a bottle of spirits a day, usually gin.

A few days before the end of the trip I became alarmed at his sudden, strange behaviour. It was his custom to come up on the bridge at ten p.m. and have a cup of tea with me before retiring. On the night in question, he arrived on time, dressed in full uniform, including his hat. I was mildly surprised as he didn't usually wear his uniform hat at sea. We had a perfectly normal and lucid chat as well as a cup of tea. Eventually he said 'Good night,' and went to bed, or so I thought. About ten minutes later he returned but this time stark naked. I have to say I was quite startled. I felt quite uncomfortable as we stood peering out of the wheelhouse windows. Once again we had a perfectly normal conversation before he said 'Good night' for the second time. You can imagine my astonishment and alarm when he appeared for a third time dressed in full uniform. Now I knew that he was in a disturbed state of mind. We chatted perfectly normally for a few minutes and then he set off for bed again. This time he didn't come back.

When the Second Mate came on the bridge at midnight, I related the events of the evening. I told him that in my estimation the skipper had gone off his rocker but the Second Mate didn't seem to be too perturbed by my story. He just advised me to go to bed and forget all about it.

My last job before retiring was to wind up a number of clocks including one in the Captain's dayroom. I walked in very quietly in view of the evening's events only to be further shocked to find the Captain flat on his back, stark naked on the floor. My first reaction was to think that he had fallen, bumped his head and was unconscious. I bent down to examine him for signs of injury. I was close to his face when suddenly his eyes shot open and stared at me. He quickly got to his feet and, looking around, grabbed an orange out of his fruit bowl, put it in my hand and shoved me out of the room.

Somewhat stunned I returned to the bridge to tell the Second Mate what had happened. 'He's off his rocker. He's definitely flipped his lid.'

Once again the Second Mate didn't seem to appreciate the seriousness of the situation. 'Well let's at least get his gun off him,' I suggested. One day I had seen him blasting away at seabirds so I knew he had a revolver. 'Look, in his strange state of mind he might blow his brains out or even worse, he might blow someone else's brains out.' But the Second Mate would have none of it, telling me to go to bed and lock my cabin door, an unnecessary instruction if ever there was one.

The next morning I went on the bridge at eight a.m. The Chief Officer updated me on the night's happenings. The Second Mate had had a very taxing watch. The Captain had been running about for hours in a very agitated state of mind; the Second Mate roused the Chief Officer, who in turn woke up the Chief Engineer and the Chief Steward. The three most senior men on the ship decided to take charge of the situation. Somehow they managed to get the Captain into his bunk and gave him an injection of morphine, which promptly put him to sleep. This was obviously a very grave and serious course of action as they were in fact taking charge of the ship, but they had little alternative. What happened next could be the subject of some dispute in terms of whether their actions were reckless, ill-advised or simply appropriate, given the circumstances. For the following two and a half days on each occasion the Captain showed any signs of waking up they gave him another shot of morphine.

We were bound for London which meant picking up a pilot at Dungeness. On the morning of picking up the pilot the three Chiefs realised that the Captain would be obliged to make an appearance on the bridge. If the pilot did not meet the Captain he would be extremely suspicious and report the matter, an action which would probably herald the end of the Captain's career. The three men decided that they had to wake him up and get him dressed, something easier said than done. We were due to pick up the pilot at about eleven a.m. during my watch. Stopping the ship and approaching the pilot boat was usually the Captain's responsibility. This morning it appeared it would be mine.

There followed a running commentary between me and the officers below.

'We've managed to wake him up.'

'Better hurry up the pilot boat is only five miles away.'

'We've got his trousers on.'

'I'm stopping the ship.'

I instructed two sailors to put a pilot ladder over the ship's side. The pilot boat came alongside and the pilot began his long climb to the bridge. There was no sign of the Captain. 'He's blown it,' I thought. 'They haven't managed to get him up here.'

What happened next left me wide-eyed, open-mouthed and flabbergasted. As the pilot walked in the port wheelhouse door, the Captain appeared at the starboard door. They met in the middle of the wheelhouse and shook hands warmly. 'My God!' said the Captain, 'am I glad to see you? I've been stuck on this bridge for three days during bad weather. She's all yours.' With that he promptly turned around and left the bridge. I was speechless. I could not believe what I had just heard. I muttered 'Good Morning,' to the pilot and he rang 'Full Ahead Engines,' and off we went.

The Captain did lose his job, though how the owners discovered his drink problem I do not know. The last I heard of him was that he was employed as a berthing pilot in Bahrain in the Persian Gulf. 'Best place for him,' I thought.

Chapter 11

Passengers and Polite Conversation

Another of the old sailing ship men's sayings was that they were only happy when on 'the lee side of Bum Island.' The full implications of this statement are perhaps best not explored except to affirm that around forty, mainly young men locked away on a ship for many months at a time creates diverse problems.

In all male communities, foul, colourful language becomes the norm. These days, obscene language has become commonplace and crossed the gender boundary, but in the 1950's and 60's it was not considered acceptable to use it when ladies were present. A man who did not show appropriate restraint in this regard could expect to be confronted by more gallant males in the vicinity. This was quite a strain for sailors who would inadvertently drop a verbal grenade into their normal conversation. This simply served to illustrate another problem; being away at sea for months, or even years, meant that when we eventually returned home, our talk of ships, cargoes and foreign places was completely alien to our relatives - and womenfolk in particular.

On some ships, if the accommodation was suitable, the Captain and the Chief Engineer were allowed to have their wives join them for the voyage. The rest of us had mixed feelings about this and had to be very careful about our use of offensive language, never knowing who might be within earshot. Most of the wives were in their fifties but their number could include a much younger woman. The effect of this upon the rest of the crew, totally starved of female company, was to significantly raise the blood pressure. The sight of a skimpily dressed or bikini clad bronzed goddess padding about the ship was disconcerting, to say the least.

Senior Officers almost always had their own bathrooms or showers. On one old trampship the Chief Engineer did not and was obliged to use a communal shower room shared by all the other engineers. This was not a problem until the Chief decided to bring his young wife along for the trip. When she wanted a shower, no one else was allowed in and the Chief would stand guard on the main door. This system worked very well until the unexpected happened one morning when the Chief told his wife that he was going for a shower, and set off with a towel wrapped around his waist. On his way he visited the engineer's messroom and became involved in some lengthy discussion about a problem in the engine room.

A few minutes after he had left his cabin the Chief's wife decided to go for a stroll. Her walk took her past the showers where the sound of cascading water indicated that her husband was still involved in his ablutions. Being a fun loving girl she thought she would play a prank on him.

The Fourth Engineer was enjoying a hot soapy shower when to his astonishment, an obviously female hand slid round the shower curtain and gently explored his masculinity with a few gentle caresses. Then a female voice enquired, 'What do you think about that then?' The Fourth Engineer knew exactly what he thought about it but decided, very wisely, to say nothing and the hand withdrew, much to his disappointment.

The Chief Engineer's wife continued her stroll, probably puzzled at having received no reply and that her husband had apparently lost his sense of humour. Passing the engineer's messroom, to her sudden horror, she saw her husband in deep conversation with some of his colleagues. She promptly fled back to her cabin and was too embarrassed to emerge for days following.

The incident caused great hilarity among the whole ship's company. The Fourth Engineer's face wore a foolish smile for days; the Chief Engineer said nothing.

You could argue, with some justification that cargo ships and tankers were not designed with women in mind. On the U.K coast some Junior Officers were allowed to have their wives onboard; on Asian crew ships with European officers even the carpenter had a kind of petty officer status. Chippy had not been married long and at the end of the voyage he was very keen to have his wife living on board. She was a very friendly and attractive lady and coming back to the ship late one night I decided to buy her a bunch of flowers. The flower seller was very tired and wanted to go home, so sold me the last of his flowers, a whole bucketful, for the price of one bunch. Fuelled by alcohol I thought nothing of carrying a large quantity of flowers on a train back to the docks. Since the hour was very late I decided to leave them outside her cabin door.

The following morning Chippy, finding a huge quantity of flowers, was not at all pleased. He wandered about the accommodation trying to find the wretch who had bought them for his wife. She, on the other hand was extremely flattered, searching the corridors to give her secret admirer a kiss if she could only discover his identity. Not wishing to be the recipient of Chippy's punch on the nose, I resolved that it would be wisest to forego his wife's kiss.

Worse was to come. Chippy, having been at sea for six months was anxious to exercise his conjugal rights. However, his attractive young wife was not of like mind, perhaps due in part to the thin plywood partitions between the cabins.

The occupant of the neighbouring cabin was a tough, Liverpudlian Chief Steward, a man who had been married for about thirty years and long forgotten the coyness or sensitivity of newlyweds. He was trying to get to sleep, but was thwarted in his attempts because of Chippy's amorous advances just a few inches beyond the plywood partition. Chippy was doing his best to woo his wife but she was having none of it.

After the pleading and rebuffs had gone on for some considerable time, the Chief Steward could stand it no longer. Suddenly he shouted, 'Oh! For God's sake missus, let him have it and then we can all get some sleep.' Any spark of passion was immediately extinguished as Chippy and his wife realized with horror that their every word was clearly audible in the next cabin.

Next morning Chippy had developed a different kind of passion – a burning desire to kill the Chief Steward. Such was the depth of ill-feeling between them that the Steward was promptly posted to another ship, his remarks considered as offensive.

It was ten 'o' clock at night when I heard the Captain's wife scream. We were in the middle of the North Atlantic and I was on watch on the bridge, right above the Captain's quarters. He was a very competent and professional man; she was a quietly spoken, well dressed and well educated lady.

A few moments later the telephone rang. It was the Captain. He was always very formal and never called me by my name. 'Third Mate? Bring my golf clubs down.' I wondered at the sanity of this request given the time and our location. For some strange reason he kept his golf clubs in the chart room and, as there was no shipping nearby, I carried his golf bag down, somewhat apprehensive of what I would find.

'Third Mate, there's a rat in my room.' he announced when I arrived.

'Oh! Where's your wife sir?'

'She's locked herself in the bedroom. I've shut all the doors so I know it's still in here somewhere. Here, take a golf club. We're going to kill it.'

I have to admit that I shudder at the thought of rats, but I can deal with them if necessary. There followed an exhaustive search which yielded no sign of the repulsive creature. The Captain was very puzzled and I was beginning to wonder whether the elusive rodent was merely a product of his imagination. Disappointed by the lack of success in our quest he had no alternative but to order me to return to the bridge, 'And if the telephone rings again, don't answer it, just come straight down.'

About twenty minutes later the peace of the bridge was shattered by another scream followed almost immediately by the urgent ring of the telephone. Down I went and grabbed my golf club.

'Damned rat must have been in the bedroom with her.'

'Oh! Where is she now sir?'

'I don't know, she's run off somewhere.'

The search which followed was both frantic and fruitless. We had scoured his quarters and now found ourselves in his dayroom feeling baffled and somewhat foolish. I was just considering returning to bridge once more when a slight movement caught my eye. Looking up I spotted the loathsome animal on top of a curtain rail. Somehow realizing that it had been seen, it took off along the rail and dived head first down the curtain to the deck. I was astonished that it was able to do this but my surprise turned to horror when the rat ran at full speed directly towards me. Instinctively I flailed at the advancing creature with my golf club and by some fluke managed to make significant contact.

I was so shocked and terrified that I was unable to stop battering it with the club. The Captain stood near me, very calmly said, 'You can stop hitting it now, Third Mate. It's quite dead; you don't need to hit it any more.' My panic slowly subsided as the Captain's words penetrated the whirl of my brain. His dignity restored, the Captain produced a dustpan, scooped up the flattened rat and dumped it unceremoniously into the ocean. For my part, I was greatly relieved to return to the tranquility of the bridge.

Ship's officers usually marry down to earth, practical women like nurses and teachers. Their wives need to be capable and independent because their husbands are away for many months of the year, leaving them with the responsibility of running the home and bringing up the children. Of necessity they often develop their own interests and circle of friends and, sometimes, this can make life difficult when their husbands appear for their occasional spells of shore leave. There was no better example of this than Tom, a trampship Chief Mate, who was known to be an excellent seaman though he had few airs and graces. He and I were great friends, often putting the world to rights as we shared a bottle of rum. Sometimes he talked about his wife, who I had never met, but was obviously quite a strong willed lady - and needed to be by all accounts, married to Tom. When he was on leave he frequently drank to excess and this led to quite a bit of friction between them because she felt his conduct humiliated her in the eyes of her friends. He was of the opinion that, although he hardly knew them, her circle of friends had a rather high opinion of themselves.

On one occasion, when he was home on leave, his wife decided to have a party to which she invited all her top-drawer friends. Tom was given strict instructions about his behaviour; he was to get smartly dressed, use no bad language and, above all, exercise due moderation in his alcohol consumption.

Initially the party went well with copious amounts of drink and a delicious variety of canapés. Tom mixed affably, beaming benignly at everyone, and joining in amiably with their smalltalk. In his language and demeanour he was the very model of self-control and his wife could not help the occasional smile of approval in his direction.

As the evening wore on the atmosphere in the room became rather stuffy and he had to discard the jacket of his smart lounge suit. He had by now consumed a considerable amount of alcohol but still felt in full command of his senses as he visited the bathroom in response to an urgent call of nature. When he slipped his braces off, unbeknown to him, they slid into the toilet pan beneath him. Dressing a few minutes later he was still completely unaware of what had happened, deciding that the damp feel to the back of his shirt was merely perspiration. Back he went to mingle with the guests.

The party ended rather abruptly as guests suddenly decided that it was time to leave for one reason or another. Tom's wife, aware of the problem, could not establish the source of the appalling smell which pervaded the room and it was only when the party had ended that she caught sight of Tom's back. The reason for her guests' premature departure was only too apparent and the verbal onslaught which followed left him in no doubt of the utter shame and humiliation he had brought upon her. Within a few days he managed to escape her wrath by returning to sea. Despite this, Tom was incapable of thinking of the incident as anything other than a huge joke.

During my seagoing career I was under the impression that there were no women employed on British merchant vessels other than very large passenger ships. I was aware that Scandinavian ships employed women, often as wireless operators, so it was quite a shock to the system when a female engineer joined the tanker on which I was serving.

Vic Drummond signed on as Second Engineer. She was a very large lady in her late fifties or early sixties, very well spoken and quite clearly the product of a public school education. I heard that she was the only female engineer in the whole British Merchant Navy. However, she spent only a few weeks with us on the UK coast and then was paid off.

About twenty years later, and by now a teacher, I was taking a school assembly when I had quite a surprise. I suddenly realised that I was reading a story to the children about a heroine called Victoria Drummond[53]. Vic, as we called her, was the first woman in the world to pass a Chief Engineer's Certificate. When she was forty years old she retired from seagoing duties and took a shore job. With the outbreak of World War Two Vic promptly volunteered to go back to sea where she played an important part in the evacuation of troops from Dunkirk. Under constant attack from German bombers, her ship made six separate channel crossings to rescue numerous exhausted and wounded British soldiers.

Vic also displayed tremendous bravery in 1941 when her ship was crossing the Atlantic from America only to be attacked by a German Condor. The first salvo of bombs was right on target and Vic, who was in the Engine Room, was blown off her feet, bruised and badly shaken. A tactic in such a situation was to increase speed and adopt an erratic zig-zag course. The ship's usual speed was nine knots but Vic pushed it up to thirteen knots which created a dangerous boiler pressure. The Condor continued to attack and so Vic ordered all of the men out of the Engine Room. On its third run the Condor was again right on target whilst steam and oil filled the Engine Room as, for forty-five minutes, Vic wrestled with the controls alone. The Condor repeatedly attacked the ship until all its bombs were used up, but even then Vic was in great danger because the boilers were threatening to explode. It was only when the speed and pressure had been reduced that she allowed engine room staff back down to take over.

When the ship got back to England, Vic was decorated for her bravery. She went to Buckingham Palace to be awarded an M.B.E and the Lloyds War Medal, the first woman to honoured with that award. Looking back now, I wish I had known all that when I sailed with her.

I had obtained a 'First Mate's Foreign Going Certificate' and was accumulating enough sea time to study for a Master Mariners Certificate. At long last I had managed to get away from trampships and tankers. I had managed to secure employment with an excellent passenger/cargo ship company. My cabin was luxurious and the food was fit for a king. I had to dress in uniform for meals and dine with the passengers and, although it was a bit of a strain, I could manage polite conversation for the duration of a meal. Despite this, we all lived on a knife edge, well aware that if we offended a passenger it would mean automatic dismissal.

For the most part the passengers were very friendly and liked to feel part of the ship's company. In port they were quick to take advantage of the crew's local knowledge even making requests for us to act as guides to the delights of the red light areas.

In really bad weather most of the passengers were too poorly to leave their cabins, but I recall one tough old lady who was never seasick and appeared for all meals. She had once been a ballerina, but was now in her seventies and quite crippled. With the aid of two sticks she managed the most amazing balancing feats, even when the ship was rolling on its beam ends. She was fiercely independent and refused all help. Her journey from her cabin to the dining saloon was a combination of zigzagging leaps, totters and jumps. She even negotiated the stairs as the ship rolled heavily. About half a dozen of us were always hovering in the background ready to catch her if her sticks slipped. Although she never fell, we always breathed a sigh of relief when she finally sat down.

In large ports like Cape Town these passenger ships were very suited to 'shippers' parties'. The purpose of these parties was to encourage the shippers to use the company to transport their goods. It was my first experience of a large gathering where all the food and drink was free and very smart waiters continuously circulated carrying trays of wine and spirits and tasty morsels of food.

These parties usually took place in the afternoon on a sunny boat deck. All the passengers, shippers, wives, girlfriends and officers turned up in their finery. Initially everyone was on good behaviour sipping drinks and chatting politely but, after about two hours the alcohol had worked its inevitable magic. The men were attempting to make off with someone else's wife or girlfriend whilst the more energetic youngsters were taking their clothes off, jumping off the boat deck to swim in the sea. How no-one drowned remains a mystery.

It was at one of these parties that Sparks managed to produce a girlfriend. Sparks, a little fat man who normally did not have much luck with the ladies, had to suffer quite a lot of ribbing which explained his usual doleful, downcast expression. Unknown to anyone, Sparks had been ashore before the Shippers' Party and met an immensely fat girl. He invited her to the party and, treating her like some kind of trophy, formally introduced her to everyone there. He was clearly very happy with his 'catch'.

During the afternoon the poor girl was overcome by the heat or, more likely, the amount of alcohol she had consumed. Sparks offered her the use of his cabin to lie down and recover whilst he returned to the party and continued to circulate. He was now on the receiving end of more teasing and a barrage of comments, 'Oh! I see your girlfriend's gone.' 'Left you has she?' 'I didn't think it would last long!' Sparks was furious, insisting I took his key to prove she was in his cabin, 'Here John. Go and have a look and tell them all she's still here.'

I was quite startled to find the girl snoring loudly. For some reason she had taken off all her clothes and was firmly wedged in his bunk. She reminded me of Queen Boudicca and I instantly determined to cover her modesty whilst preserving her regal appearance. Running up onto the Bridge I selected a crisp new Red Ensign which, once I had returned to the cabin, I draped quite artistically around her. She never stirred.

Within the next half hour Sparks gave his cabin key to almost everyone to prove she had not left. Unfortunately this only led to more ribald comments. 'Bloody Hell! Sparks! How did you manage to get in the bunk with her?' 'Did you need a pair of step ladders to get on top of her?'

Eventually Sparks returned to his cabin and, to his great wrath, discovered the flag. He came back to the party in an evil mood, determined to seek retribution. 'Right then, who touched her? Who put that bloody flag on her? I'll kill the bastard when I find out.' Luckily, he never did find out and the following day even saw the funny side of it himself.

After dinner, in warm sunny weather, coffee and liqueurs would be served on the boatdeck. These were occasions for the Captain and passengers only, but a prank in which I was involved was to make one such event truly memorable.

The Second Officer, Sparks and I were all good friends. Our cabins were on the same level as the boatdeck and I think it would be fair to say the three of us were slightly mad. This particular Sparks was an elderly, well-educated Scot who could be a bit toffee-nosed at times. He hinted that he had private means and only came to sea for the company and to keep himself occupied. He enjoyed a tipple like the rest of us and at some point in the jollifications he felt the need to become a 'ballerina'. He would skip away and return in long thermal underwear to entertain us with hilarious but quite skilful dancing.

Bill, the Second Officer was a great prankster and I was usually on the receiving end of his tricks. In South Africa we had acquired two African killing sticks called knobkerries and two woolly hats. A drinking session usually ended up with the pair of us fencing and jousting with our knobkerries.

One evening, after one or two aperitifs, I planned revenge on Bill after having fallen victim to another of his pranks. Bill was in the shower and I was dressed only in a towel because I had completed mine. I had managed to obtain a bucket of putrid bilge water which I balanced on top of the door of Bill's shower and waited. My trick worked perfectly; Bill was covered in the foul mess. I had a fair idea of what his reaction would be so I was already wearing my woolly hat and armed with my knobkerrie. An enraged Bill grabbed his hat and stick and came after me hollering like a deranged Zulu as I made off along the boat deck. Semi-naked, towels waving, killing sticks twirling dangerously, we were in headlong career along the deck.

Unfortunately we had both forgotten about the civilised gathering, sipping drinks at the end of the boat deck. Bill and I came haring round the corner, right through the middle of the Captain and passengers. I think they might have had some warning from Bill's near hysterical bellowing but nevertheless, chaos resulted. Tables, chairs, passengers, drinks and Captain went flying in all directions. Luckily, by some miracle Bill and I did not lose our footing. In a split second we both made the same rather cowardly decision not to stop and offer apologies. We continued, now silently, up the starboard side of the boat deck back to Bill's cabin. We sat there, horrified at the enormity of what we had done.

The Captain was a huge, impressive looking man of few words with whom we had a purely professional relationship - though he trusted us implicitly. By the time he visited us we were sitting shamefaced like two naughty boys. He gave us a long, hard, withering look until,finally he spoke, 'You're both sacked.' He then turned on his heel and disappeared. The subject was never mentioned again and we never found out what the passengers thought of our antics.

Of course he'd sacked us on a previous occasion and reinstated us. Luckily we were both thoroughly experienced deck officers and good at our jobs.

As I mentioned earlier, each officer was required to sit with a group of passengers at mealtimes. At breakfast I had noticed with fascination a gentleman who cut off the top of his boiled egg with a knife. It seemed much more efficient than my method, which was to beat the top of the egg with a teaspoon, then pick off the pieces of shell. After watching the man for a few days, I decided to try it myself, with disastrous consequences. The first two attempts failed completely and I decided, losing my patience, that more force was required. My grip on the egg, coupled with the pressure of the knife, caused the egg to effectively explode, shooting its bright yellow liquid yolk across the crisp white tablecloth. I was extremely embarrassed, a discomfort not helped by some silent, disapproving glances.

My faux pas however was not as bad as the one I heard a few days later. Sometimes there is a lull in general conversation during which one person's voice becomes suddenly prominent. Just such an event had occurred and the lone voice on this occasion belonged to the Chief Engineer, sitting with three dear old ladies who were hanging on his every word. Speaking in a rather loftily superior voice he was saying 'Do you know ladies? Science is such a wonderful thing. When I'm wearing my glasses I can see a ship twenty miles away. Take them off and I can't see a f*****g thing.' Everyone heard. There was a kind of stunned silence. The dear old ladies tut tutted their disapproval. The Chief Engineer didn't order the next course and left explaining that he had a problem in the Engine Room to attend to.

Unfortunately, science was not serving me quite so well. The continual use of sextant, binoculars, azimuth mirror and dazzling tropical sunshine was taking its toll on my eyes. I was unaware of any problem and did not need glasses. Whilst being examined for a First Mate's Certificate I had the usual MOT eyesight test. A few days later I received a letter telling me my eyesight was near borderline failure level, and that if there was any further deterioration in my vision I would not be allowed back at sea.

I carried on to pass the First Mate's Certificate but was now in a serious predicament. It would take me at the least, three years to accumulate enough sea time experience to sit a Master Mariner's Certificate by which time I might be barred from going to sea anymore. What was I to do? There were other concerns too. Being employed by a very good shipping company meant that promotion was very slow and future prospects did not look good. Other men were spending six years on the twelve to four watch as Second Officer, twenty years on the four to eight watch as Chief Officer and about five years as Captain before retiring. I was also totally unaware at the time that, in the years ahead, the British Merchant Fleet was destined to shrink from its then complement of six thousand ocean going vessels to the few hundred of the present time.

I went back to sea for three years and mulled over the problem. When I had accumulated enough sea time for the next certificate I came ashore. I still had no need of reading glasses nor was I experiencing any problems. However, I just did not dare to take the required eyesight test because, if I failed that, it would be the end of my career.

I decided to look for alternative shore based employment but retaining the opportunity of going back to sea. Unfortunately, having gone to a sea school and being apprenticed at sixteen I had no 'O' or 'A' level GCE's. Nobody understood my nautical qualifications so they were of no use when I applied for jobs. I finally decided that I wanted to be a teacher but how would I manage to get into a teacher training college? I set to and studied for a variety of GCE's, both at 'O' and 'A' levels.

Using correspondence courses and evening classes I eventually gained the necessary qualifications.

Making the transition from a sea life to a shore life was extremely difficult. For about three years I was a social misfit but well aware of what was going on. I had spoken to many men who had tried to 'swallow the anchor' but had failed. During this period I had many different jobs, working variously as a docker, taxi driver, factory worker, on a strawberry farm and at a Butlins Holiday Camp. To fund my teacher training I returned to sea for short spells. It is rather absurd really; I do really need glasses now but as I have never failed an eyesight test there is nothing to stop me from going back to sea. Why were there such stringent regulations about vision anyway? People wearing spectacles can see perfectly well and, because of my training, I can still see a speck on the sea horizon before anyone else.

Fifty years on, have I got the sea out of my blood? No. I still experience a yearning to feel a heaving deck underneath my feet again. But common sense prevails. I well recollect the tough life on a trampship, the boring voyages on tankers and the twenty four hour discomfort of a North Atlantic storm.

To alleviate the magnetism of the sea I have always felt the need to live close to the coast. I do however, get great pleasure from wild moors, hills and mountains. For about twenty-years my sport was sub-aqua diving and I continue to mess about with small motorboats, inflatables, RIBs and sailing dinghies.

I often wonder what I would do if I had my youth over again. The sea life is character building, but some would say the converse is true and see it as destructive. On the other hand, I met people I admired tremendously; I saw spectacular sights at sea and visited fascinating countries; I have vivid memories which remind me that I have lived life to the full.

But, would I go to sea again at the age of sixteen? With the benefit of hindsight, I can say that my answer is a resounding 'Not bloody likely!'

Nautical Glossary and Bibliography

1. Ballast- heavy material (usually water) taken onboard to get an empty vessel lower and more stable in the water.
2. Knot- a unit of speed equivalent to one nautical mile (6080ft) per hour.
3. Sextant- an optical instrument usually used to measure the angle of the sun, planets and stars above the horizon.
4. Azimuth- an optical instrument mounted on top of a compass, used to find the direction of celestial and terrestrial objects.
5. Gyro compass- a man-made compass that does not use magnetism to find north.
6. Bosun- in charge of the sailors. Equivalent to a foreman.
7. Watch- four hour spell of duty onboard a ship- 12-4, 4-8, 8-12.
8. Bunkering- taking on fuel for the engines.
9. Starboard- The right hand side of a ship when looking towards the bows. Port the left hand side.
10. Hatch- an opening in the deck through which cargo is lowered into the hold.
11. Bilge- a compartment in the bottom of a ship's hold where rotting material and liquids collect.
12. Derrick- a crane on the deck for lifting cargo.
13. Bulkhead- any kind of partition separating ship's cabins or water-tight compartments.
14. Winch- an engine used in conjunction with a derrick to lift or lower heavy objects.
15. Saloon- dining room.
16. Irish horse- slang for tough meat.
17. Galley- cookhouse.
18. Hard tack- slang for poor food.

19. Old man- the Captain is invariably referred to as the 'old man', but not to his face.
20. Clyde Puffer- a small steam powered cargo vessel used on the Clyde and Western Isles of Scotland.
21. Windlass- an engine like a winch used for heaving up the anchor or tightening mooring ropes.
22. Bollards- strong posts used to secure mooring ropes.
23. Poop- stern area of a ship.
24. Aft- towards the stern.
25. Forud- towards the bow of a ship.
26. Flying bridge- an elevated walkway on a tanker to provide safe movement from one part of the ship to another.
27. First dog watch- 4a.m. to 6a.m.
28. Second dog watch- 6a.m. to 8a.m.
29. Half seas over- drunk.
30. Helm- ship's wheel for steering.
31. Hard-a-starboard- putting the rudder as far right as it will go.
32. Beam- at right angles to the direction the vessel is going, or on her beam ends- on her side almost capsizing.
33. Hove to- a vessel is stopped.
34. Foc'sal head- from forecastle, the very front of the ship.
35. Wheel- the ship's steering wheel.
36. Telegraph- an instrument on the bridge used to send engine requirements e.g. full ahead, to the engine room.
37. Wide berth- keep well clear of.
38. Wake- turbulence behind the ship made by the propeller.
39. Bottlescrew- a device by which wire stays can be tightened.
40. Batten down the hatches- cover the hatches to prevent water getting into the holds.
41. Roadstead- safe anchorage.
42. Freeboard- distance between the waterline and the top of the ship's side.
43. Hatch coaming- the top edge of the hatch opening.
44. Cluster- portable bright electric light.
45. Belaying pin- a wooden or metal pin, normally stuck through a rail, to which a rope can be secured quickly.
46. Block- a pulley fitted in a frame.
47. Sparks- the nickname given to all wireless operators.
48. Aweigh- the moment the anchor lifts off the seabed.
49. Truck- a wooden disc fitted to the very top of the mast.
50. Chippy- a nickname given to all ship's carpenters.

51. Fluke- a triangular plate on the end of the arm of an anchor designed to dig into the seabed.
52. Bosun's chair- a wooden seat on the end of a sling of rope enabling a man to be hauled up the mast or lowered over the ship's side.
53. Primary School Assemblies, Frank L Pinfold, Ward Lock Educational.

Lightning Source UK Ltd.
Milton Keynes UK
UKOW05f0308160617
303474UK00001B/50/P